A Beginner's Guide to
Japanese Tea

A Beginner's Guide to Japanese Tea

SELECTING AND BREWING THE PERFECT CUP
OF SENCHA, MATCHA AND OTHER JAPANESE TEAS

Per Oscar Brekell

TUTTLE Publishing

Tokyo | Rutland, Vermont | Singapore

Contents

Introduction

The Joys of Japanese Tea

If I were to describe the joys of Japanese tea in only a few words, I would say that by taking just one sip the sweet fragrance immerses the heart and mind in tranquility, conjuring the subtle beauty and elegant simplicity of a tea garden's remote mountain setting.

In Japan, the saying *shichu no sankyo,* or "a mountain dwelling in the city," summarizes a concept prevalent since the age of the Higashiyama culture. Great tea masters like Sen No Rikyu, who shaped the Japanese tea ceremony, constructed tea houses that, even if located in a bustling city center, could summon the quiet and secluded life of the mountains, creating a space where our minds can be temporarily freed from the strains and struggles of everyday life.

I believe that this saying aptly summarizes the true beauty of Japanese tea. Even if you happen to be in the middle of a bustling metropolis, the aroma that rises from your cup invigorates you, creating a peace of mind and serenity as if you were standing in the middle of a tea garden surrounded by misty forested slopes.

In fact, the beauty of Japanese tea stretches far beyond that. Although bitterness, astringency and sweetness are elements that you can find in other teas as well, the strong emphasis on *umami* is a true characteristic of Japanese tea. The Japanese word *umami* is now incorporated in many languages and is a natural element not only in Japanese cuisine but is universally recognized as one of the five basic tastes. It is, however, very rare to find it in beverages. I believe those distinct flavors make Japanese tea stand out when compared to tea from other countries.

Japanese tea can be prepared in many ways using either cold or hot water. The steeping method can be adjusted both to bring out a perfect balance of all its taste elements and to highlight a specific flavor. You can, for example, choose to either accentuate *umami* or bring out as

Having become an integral part of Japanese society, tea was then reshaped over hundreds of years, eventually turning into something distinctly Japanese, reflecting the unique sentiment and traditions of the Far Eastern island nation.

much of the aroma as possible. The tea can be adjusted to anyone's taste or to the season. Therefore, it perfectly embodies the concept of Japanese hospitality, or *omotenashi*, putting all your effort into the comfort and well-being of your guest. A tea whose taste and flavor changes depending on the steeping technique may sound difficult to manage at first, but once you learn the basics the possibilities are endless and you will come to enjoy the steeping process. In your quest for a good cup of tea, you will find a strong ally in the Japanese teapot, which is both easy to use and makes the tea taste better. Japanese teaware not only leads the way to a better cup of tea, but these utensils, shaped and improved by a long history and a rich cultural heritage, also add depth and beauty to your tea experience.

Since both Japanese food culture and the culture of *omotenashi* look to the importance of tea, it also allows us to enjoy and savor the essence of Japanese culture. Culture is not just about preserving the traditions of the past but something that lives inside us, and based on the

wisdom of the past and our current actions it constantly continues to evolve. The tea that we are drinking today is very different in taste, flavor and appearance from the tea we drank in the past. Thanks to progress in processing and manufacturing, the Japanese tea that is produced comes close to the ideal green tea, having the characteristic fresh aroma while at the same time being strong in *umami*. Another change is that quality tea is no longer the province of the upper echelons of society. Today, everyone can enjoy the very best teas. Just like single vineyard wine or single malt whiskey, more and more people are discovering the unique and varied taste experiences of single estate Japanese tea, which first appeared at the beginning of the 21st century.

In countries other than Japan, perhaps due to their relative unfamiliarity with green tea and different water qualities that do not do justice to the original taste, there is still a tendency to emphasize the health benefits rather than the taste and flavor of the tea. Of course, I also believe that drinking green tea

Brewing tea allows for a moment of tranquility and peace. Having mastered the basic principles, you will be able to tune the taste to your own preferences.

promotes health. However, rather than drinking Japanese tea to prolong one's life, I would like to think of it as something that makes our time on earth richer and more enjoyable. Life is full of hardships and we always encounter both foreseen and unforeseen troubles that cause stress in our everyday lives. But by drinking Japanese tea we get a moment of peace and are able to gain the strength we need to remain positive in the midst of stress and strain. Even during good times, we can share our feelings and deepen our understanding of one another over a cup of green tea. I sincerely hope that by reading this book more people will be encouraged to lead rich and fulfilling lives with the subtle beauty of Japanese tea as a part of it. Welcome to the wonderful world of Japanese tea!

Chapter One

What is Japanese Tea?

Japan produces many different kinds of tea, including black tea, oolong tea, pan-fired green tea and, to a lesser extent, fermented tea. However, the production volumes of the fermented varieties are comparatively small, and therefore in Japan they are usually referred to as local specialties or rare teas rather than "Japanese tea." Most tea produced in Japan is green tea.

When processing green tea, the fresh leaves are heated or steamed to deactivate the enzymes, thereby preventing oxidation. Dry heat is the primary method used outside Japan. Steaming is essentially a Japanese method that contributes significantly to a unique Japanese taste experience.

Japanese teas are processed to preserve the natural taste and flavor of the fresh leaves, thereby changing the chemical compounds as little as possible. In this sense, Japanese tea is quite different from both oxidized tea like black tea and pan-fired green tea, allowing for tastes and flavors that cannot be achieved elsewhere.

Another attribute peculiar to Japanese tea, which is also found in Japanese food culture, in general, is the pursuit of and emphasis on *umami* rather than aroma. Perhaps Japanese tea lacks grandiose characteristics, but after having learned to appreciate it the hidden beauty wrapped in the neatly rolled leaves becomes apparent.

Since both freshness and savory flavor are sought after and praised as important characteristics of tea and Japanese cuisine overall, the country's food culture is reflected in its tea. The fresh aroma induces a feeling of richness, and since the taste and flavor change according to the chosen steeping method, new brewing discoveries can constantly be made.

The Essential Elements of Japanese Teas

Umami

As with Japanese food, the word *umami* has also crossed borders and spread throughout the world. Usually described as the sensation of richness or savoriness in food, it is a taste element that makes Japanese tea truly unique. Ichibancha, tea from the first harvest, is rich in *umami* and considered to be of high quality, whereas tea that has less of it, in general, is considered to be of lower quality. *Umami* is a significant determining factor when grading Japanese tea. Glutamic acid and L-theanine, the main compounds that help create the *umami* sensation, dissolve easily even when the tea is steeped at a low temperature.

Bitterness

Bitterness may sound unappetizing on its own, but it is an important taste element in tea just as it is in coffee and dark chocolate. Caffeine and catechins play the main role here, and these compounds are more easily dissolved in hot water. Therefore, it is important to cool down the water when steeping Japanese tea to prevent excess bitterness from completely taking over the taste. Catechins are the main taste components in green tea.

Astringency

Some confuse astringency with bitterness. Unlike bitterness, which is considered one of the basic five taste elements (together with sweetness, sourness, saltiness and *umami*), astringency is a tactile sensation. That dry astringent feeling in the mouth is created as the polyphenols in tea attach to proteins in our saliva. Astringency is essential to the enjoyment of tea, resulting in a pleasant aftertaste that lasts long after the tea has been swallowed.

Sweetness

L-theanine is the main compound responsible for sweetness in tea. It dissolves easily in lukewarm or cold water and therefore sweetness can be accentuated by lowering the water temperature. Sweetness compounds also dissolve faster than astringency and bitterness, which makes the first steeping rich in natural sweetness and enjoyable on its own, without any accompanying dessert or confection. Apart from L-theanine, some free sugars also add to the sweetness in tea, but there is no need to worry about any calorie intake as it is close to zero.

The Aromas and Active Ingredients of Japanese Teas

Japanese steamed green tea is often considered to be all about enjoying *umami*, yet it has a refreshing forest-like aroma that makes it stand out from other teas. One notable variety is *shincha* ("new tea," or gently finish-fired *ichiban-cha*), rich in the green leaf volatiles that contribute to this characteristic aroma.

The floral and fruity notes peculiar to certain cultivars (clones) of the tea plant are also present. Aroma compounds are volatile and sensitive to heat, so in order to produce a tea that is rich in aroma it is necessary to make the heating and drying processes as short and efficient as possible. To prevent oxidation, steam is used to fix, or denature, the enzymes in the tea so as not to scorch the leaves. Therefore, steaming is a crucial step that gives the tea its typical Japanese aroma and character.

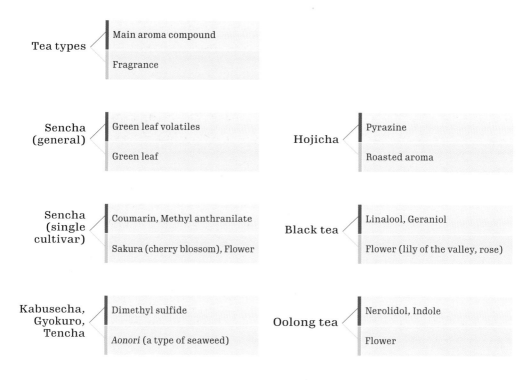

Tea types	Main aroma compound
	Fragrance

Sencha (general)	Green leaf volatiles
	Green leaf

Hojicha	Pyrazine
	Roasted aroma

Sencha (single cultivar)	Coumarin, Methyl anthranilate
	Sakura (cherry blossom), Flower

Black tea	Linalool, Geraniol
	Flower (lily of the valley, rose)

Kabusecha, Gyokuro, Tencha	Dimethyl sulfide
	Aonori (a type of seaweed)

Oolong tea	Nerolidol, Indole
	Flower

Catechin

Antioxidant

Caffeine

Stimulant

Theanine

Relaxing

Saponin

Antiviral

Japanese steamed green tea is different from tea from other countries in its taste, flavor and appearance due to the chemical compounds in the tea. The main compounds responsible for bitterness and astringency are a group of polyphenols called catechins, while caffeine also contributes to the bitter taste of tea. In Japan, catechins are considered to be a powerful antioxidant, and by protecting against gene mutation are also thought to slow down the aging process and prevent the formation of cancer cells.

L-theanine, usually credited for the sweetness and *umami* in tea, is reported to promote alpha-wave activity in the brain, making us feel calm and peaceful. Tea also contains a well-known stimulant, caffeine, which may seem contradictory, but the sensation of being both alert and relaxed without feeling any stress or nervousness probably arises from the effects of both compounds working together. Rather than consuming tea for its medicinal properties, enjoying good-tasting tea on an everyday basis provides a respite from routine and enriches our everyday life. Not being too particular about the intake of certain compounds, but instead enjoying good tea as a habit, is probably the healthiest approach to tea.

The Various Types of Teas

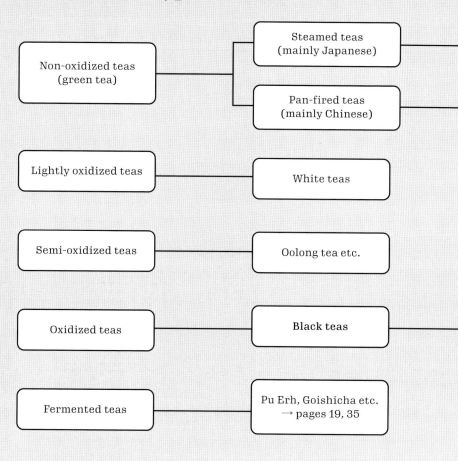

Non-oxidized teas (green tea) → Steamed teas (mainly Japanese)

Non-oxidized teas (green tea) → Pan-fired teas (mainly Chinese)

Lightly oxidized teas → White teas

Semi-oxidized teas → Oolong tea etc.

Oxidized teas → Black teas

Fermented teas → Pu Erh, Goishicha etc. → pages 19, 35

Black tea, oolong and green tea are all made from the leaves and buds and, in some cases, the stems of the tea plant (*Camellia sinensis*). The difference in aroma, taste and appearance is the result of specific styles of processing and the degree of oxidation the leaves undergo. Oxidation is prevented by deactivating enzymes in the tea leaf, a process called *sassei* in Japanese (written with the Chinese characters "kill" and "blue/green" and usually referred to as "fixing" or "kill-green" in English). There are several ways of deactivating the oxidation enzymes, and green tea will end up differently depending on the fixing method. Green tea can be divided into two main types: pan-fired green tea (usually heated in a pan or a tumbler) and steamed green tea. The former type is mainly produced in China and Taiwan and the latter mainly

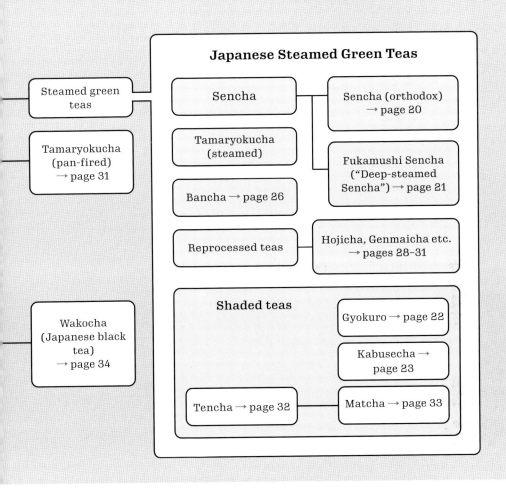

Japanese Steamed Green Teas

Steamed green teas

Tamaryokucha (pan-fired) → page 31

Wakocha (Japanese black tea) → page 34

Sencha

- Sencha (orthodox) → page 20
- Fukamushi Sencha ("Deep-steamed Sencha") → page 21

Tamaryokucha (steamed)

Bancha → page 26

Reprocessed teas

- Hojicha, Genmaicha etc. → pages 28–31

Shaded teas

- Gyokuro → page 22
- Kabusecha → page 23
- Tencha → page 32
- Matcha → page 33

in Japan. Pan-fired green teas tend to be light-bodied and have a distinct, slightly sweet roasted aroma. Steamed green teas, on the other hand, have a characteristic fresh aroma, strong *umami* and a pleasant astringency. These teas can be further divided into non-shaded and shaded teas. In the case of shaded teas like gyokuro, kabusecha and tencha (which is used to make matcha), the plantation is covered before harvest to prevent exposure to direct sunlight. Among non-shaded teas are sencha and its cousin fukamushi sencha, which is steamed and processed longer than sencha, giving it a broken appearance. Other teas include pu erh (from China), fermented by the action of microorganisms. Thus, the same *Camellia sinensis* plant can be used in various ways to produce teas that are different in taste, flavor and appearance.

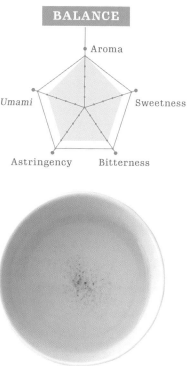

Aroma

Umami

Sweetness

Astringency

Bitterness

Sencha 煎茶

Sencha is one of the true classics in the repertoire of Japanese tea. It stands out as a tea that can be steeped and enjoyed in various ways to evoke or accentuate different flavors. In this sense, it is probably more flexible than any other tea. When using cold water, the natural sweetness of the tea is accentuated, and if water with a high temperature is used, bitterness, astringency and aroma are dissolved to a greater extent. There is no correct answer to the question of how you should steep your tea, so learning the logic behind tea steeping and then trying to apply it in different ways is by far the best approach. Ranging from blends with a good balance of both taste and flavor to unique single estate teas—which can all be enjoyed in many different ways—the world of sencha is endlessly fascinating. Since sencha is grown without shading, the natural flavor from the terroir (terrain, soil and climate conditions) and the cultivar remains, making it an excellent choice for the aficionado who likes comparing different teas in a way similar to wine or whiskey tasting.

How to steep Sencha → pages 92, 96, 100

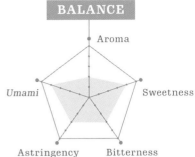

BALANCE

Aroma

Umami · · · · · Sweetness

Astringency · Bitterness

Fukamushi Sencha "Deep-Steamed Sencha" 深蒸し煎茶

Teas referred to as fukamushi sencha (usually translated as "deep-steamed sencha" or "heavily steamed sencha") all share a broken appearance and a cloudy **liquor**. Rather than aroma, fukamushi sencha is sought for its thick and rich taste and full mouthfeel. The steaming process is longer than for sencha, and it is during the rolling process that the tea gets its broken appearance. Tea grown in flat areas with long daylight hours tends to become bitter, but by steaming the leaves for a longer time, pectin—a compound that enhances sweetness—dissolves more easily, and thus fukamushi sencha is perceived as a mild tea. The processing method was developed in the 1960s in the central part of Shizuoka prefecture. Nowadays, fukamushi sencha is the most widely consumed tea in Japan. To avoid any harsh taste or excess bitterness, it should be steeped in water about 70 °C (160 °F) for best results.

How to steep Sencha → pages 92, 100
How to choose a teapot → page 116

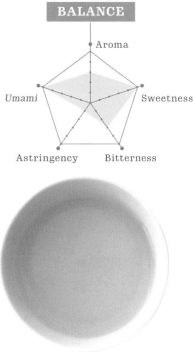

BALANCE

Aroma

Umami

Sweetness

Astringency

Bitterness

Gyokuro "Jewel Dewdrop Tea" 玉露茶

Enjoying *umami* is often considered an essential part of Japanese tea drinking, and gyokuro is one of the teas where this quality is on maximum display. Only about 250 tons are produced every year, a small amount compared to other teas. The rich *umami* does not come about by chance. Although processed in a way similar to sencha, gyokuro is grown under very different circumstances. About three weeks before the spring harvest, the tea plants are shaded using either a reed screen with straw spread on top or a synthetic black cloth to prevent exposure to direct sunlight. As the leaves grow, shading prevents the *umami* compound L-theanine from turning into catechin, a group of polyphenols that make the tea taste bitter and astringent. This and meticulous fertilizing of the tea garden are the secrets behind the strong *umami*. Gyokuro is best steeped at low temperatures, but because of its almost overwhelming richness is best enjoyed in small quantities. It also makes an excellent cold brew.

How to steep Gyokuro → pages 97, 104

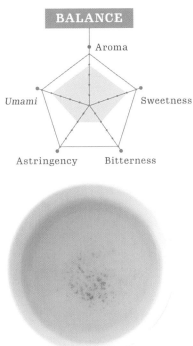

BALANCE

Aroma

Umami — Sweetness

Astringency — Bitterness

Kabusecha "Shaded Tea" かぶせ茶

Since kabusecha possesses elements found in both sencha and gyokuro, it is often described as something of a hybrid or combination of the two. Kabuse translates as "cover" in Japanese, and as the term suggests the plants are grown under shade, a cultivation method shared with gyokuro, although kabusecha is shaded for a shorter period. Unlike gyokuro, where poles hold up a reed screen roof that is later covered by straw to let the tea plant grow freely, kabusecha plantations are shaped into hedges and a synthetic black cloth put directly on the plants 4–10 days before harvest. By shading the plantation like this, the tea becomes stronger in sweetness and weaker in astringency. The characteristic nori/seaweed-like aroma is also produced, which clearly sets it apart from sencha. Kabusecha tastes good even when steeped at relatively high temperatures.

How to steep Kabusecha → page 92

23

Sencha and Bancha

First, Second, Third and Fourth Harvest Teas

Tender spring buds destined to become sencha are plucked carefully and transported to the tea factory as quickly as possible. After steaming, they are rolled and dried into their characteristic "pine needle" shape

When considering black tea or oolong tea, the teas from different seasons are appreciated for their specific character-istics. However, in the case of steamed Japanese tea, *ichibancha* (first-harvest tea) is considered to be the best, the quality incomparable to the other har-vests. There are several reasons for this. First, after waking up from winter dormancy, the absorbed nutrients end up in soft, tender buds rich in *umami* compounds. Second, since the spring buds grow at an even pace, it is easier to pick leaves with a similar shape and size. They can then be rolled into their characteristic needle-like shapes, turning the leaves into a high-quality

sencha that looks as good as it tastes.

Nibancha (second-harvest tea) and later harvests are weaker in *umami*. The leaves also become more fibrous and hard and do not grow as evenly as those of ichibancha. After processing, the non-glossy side ends up as the surface of the dried leaves. The hardness of the leaves also results in a slightly flatter

appearance. Thus, the leaves do not yield the same rich taste as ichibancha. *Sanbancha* (third-harvest tea) and *yonbancha* (fourth-harvest tea) get even more fibrous and are traded at lower prices. Tea from these harvests is generally used for making hojicha or as a base for the beverages sold in plastic bottles that are widely consumed in Japan. However, if the plantation is well-tended and the producer especially skilled, even nibancha can provide a good flavor experience. Since it has less *umami,* it can be enjoyed as a light and refreshing tea, tasting good even when steeped in slightly hot water.

BALANCE

Aroma

Umami

Sweetness

Astringency

Bitterness

Bancha 番茶

Bancha is probably one of the most confusing terms in the Japanese tea world. In preindustrial days, it referred to the low-quality, inexpensive teas consumed by commoners as opposed to matcha and high-quality leaf teas that only higher-ranking members of society could afford. This sort of bancha was processed in a variety of ways, for example, boiled or roasted over an open fire before the drying process began. Nowadays, the term bancha is mainly used to denote sencha from the second harvest and after. The bancha of old times has disappeared almost entirely and is now referred to as "rural bancha." Since it is not strong in *umami* and does not match ichibancha in color and appearance, it is often thought of as a low-grade tea, but a light-bodied bancha can be the perfect choice after a meal as it both clears the palate and refreshes the mind.

How to steep Bancha → page 110

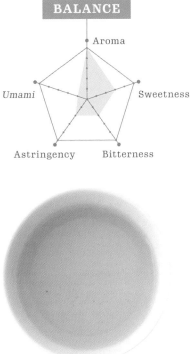

BALANCE

Aroma

Umami

Sweetness

Astringency

Bitterness

Kyobancha 京番茶

This tea from Kyoto also goes by other names, such as iribancha ("roasted bancha"). Its light, bulky brown appearance sets it worlds apart from ordinary bancha. Even Japanese unfamiliar with it might mistake it for tea from another country. After leaves for gyokuro and tencha (the base for matcha) have been picked, the plants are cut down to just below knee height to prepare them for the next year's first harvest. The leaves and branches that are cut off during this step are used for kyobancha. They are steamed, dried without rolling, stored and then roasted before being sent to market. Because of its distinctly smoky aroma and unusual appearance, many think of kyobancha as a rare tea, but until the 1920s and 1930s many teas similar to it were probably widely consumed in Japan as bancha.

How to steep Kyobancha → page 110

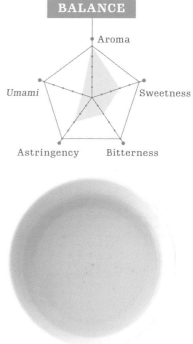

BALANCE

Aroma

Umami — Sweetness

Astringency — Bitterness

Hojicha ほうじ茶

Hojicha is made by roasting steamed green tea, and in general tea from the second harvest or after is used as a base. It is sought after for its sweet fragrance and roasted aroma. Depending on the base, hojicha can be different in both taste and flavor. Hojicha made from stems tends to be light-bodied with a sweet fragrance, whereas a leaf-based hojicha is stronger overall, with a prominent astringency. In Japan, it is mainly drunk after meals. If you happen to have sencha that has been around for a while and has gone stale, you can turn it into hojicha by carefully dry roasting it in a skillet free of any cooking residue. This will not only revive the tea but also fill your kitchen with a pleasant roasted tea aroma.

How to steep Hojicha → page 110

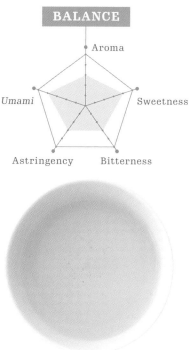

BALANCE

Aroma

Umami

Sweetness

Astringency

Bitterness

Kukicha "Stem Tea" 茎茶

Kukicha, also called bocha, is made from stems and stalks that are sifted from *aracha* (unrefined tea) by the wholesaler when steamed green teas are refined. It is commonly referred to as "twig tea" in English, a term that is slightly misleading as it might give the impression that the tea is made from stripped branches of the tea plant, which it is not. Because it is not made for its own sake but is a byproduct beverage, there are no statistics on production volume. The vegetal notes suggesting grassy plains are characteristic of kukicha. Weak in astringency, it can be steeped at slightly higher temperatures as well. This is an advantage when you are pairing it with food or would like to warm yourself on a cold winter day. When hojicha is made from kukicha, it is usually called bo hojicha or kuki hojicha.

The importance of tea refining in Japan → pages 40–41
How to steep Kukicha and Bocha → page 100

BALANCE

Aroma

Umami

Sweetness

Astringency

Bitterness

Konacha 粉茶

Konacha is a fixture at Japanese sushi restaurants because it goes well with dishes that include raw fish. Steeped in boiling water, it not only clears and refreshes the palate but the catechins it contains may also lower the risk of food poisoning. Just like kukicha, konacha is a byproduct of the sifting process during refining. The light parts (green tea dust or fannings) that are sifted and sorted end up as konacha. Due to its comparably low price, it often ends up as a teabag tea. It is often confused with powdered green tea (funmatsucha) but that is a type of tea that is ground, which makes it very different from konacha.

How to steep Konacha → page 110

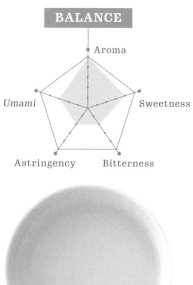

BALANCE

Aroma

Umami

Sweetness

Astringency

Bitterness

Kamairicha "Pan-fired Tea" 釜炒り茶

Almost all teas in Japan are made by steaming the fresh leaves,
whereas pan firing is usually referred to as the Chinese way of
processing green tea. Japanese pan-fired teas trace their origin
to China which has a longer history than sencha. Today, Japanese
pan-fired teas are mainly produced in the prefectures of Miyazaki
and Saga on the island of Kyushu in the southern part of Japan, and
the resulting taste is different from their Chinese cousins. You can
sense a very Japanese touch of *umami* but with less astringency
than sencha and the distinct sweet-roasted aroma refreshes both
the palate and the mind. Pan-fired Japanese teas are often called
tamaryokucha but should not be confused with steamed tamaryokucha, which is produced in a way similar to sencha but with
the last rolling step omitted.

How to steep Kamairicha → page 93

Tencha 碾茶

Apart from those who live in regions where tencha is produced, few consumers know about it. Tencha is ground, usually in a stone mill, and turned into the bright green powdered tea called matcha. It is therefore difficult to find in its original form. Tencha is shaded before harvest, just like gyokuro, but processed in a completely different way. After steaming, it is dried fast at a high temperature without rolling, after which not only the stems but also the other hard parts, including the veins, are separated from the leaves. The result is a flaky tea resembling fish scale. High-quality tencha is picked by hand during the first harvest, while mechanically harvested tencha from later seasons, processed under very different circumstances, can also be found for sale. It becomes what is often referred to as culinary matcha, usually used for sweets and pastries. Finding some high-quality tencha will benefit anyone who wants to be able to distinguish good matcha from lower grades.

BALANCE

Aroma · Sweetness · Bitterness · Astringency · Umami

Matcha 抹茶

Matcha, one of the oldest types of tea in Japan, has in recent years gained in popularity as an ingredient in confections, even overseas. Traditionally, however, it was dissolved in hot water and drunk on occasions like the Japanese tea ceremony. Tencha ground in a tea mill is considered to be proper matcha, so both its cultivation and processing differ greatly from sencha. When whisked, high-quality matcha yields a vivid deep green color and the rich aroma, combined with a strong *umami* and sweetness balanced with a pleasant astringency, create a bowl of perfect harmony. High-quality matcha can be enjoyed with a more intense flavor as koicha (thick matcha, where more powder and less water are used) or in a lighter version as usucha (light matcha, where less powder is used). Any tea lover should definitely try both. Using a traditional tea whisk (*chasen*), and enjoying the tea from a genuine Japanese bowl makes for the best experience.

How to whisk Matcha → page 106

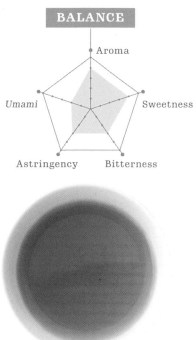

BALANCE

Aroma

Umami

Sweetness

Astringency

Bitterness

Japanese Black Tea 国産紅茶

Few associate Japan with black tea, but from the Meiji period (1868–1912) until
the middle of the Showa period (1926–1989) some of the tea producing regions
in Japan were engaged in large-scale black tea production, mainly for export.
Seeds from Indian tea plants that produced black tea were brought to Japan and
their cultivation led to new crossbreeds. Benifuki and benihikari, two cultivars
that have received attention in recent years, are examples of offspring that
share genetic material with the black tea cultivars once widely grown. After the
liberalization of the black tea trade in Japan, which coincided with a growing
domestic demand for green tea, black tea production in Japan became less
competitive and, as a result, was set on a path that almost led to its extinction.
However, in recent years Japanese black tea, or *wakocha*, as it is often called,
has seen a revival, and the mild sweet taste with almost no astringency makes it
different from tea from classic black tea countries like Sri Lanka. It tastes good
as it is without any added milk or sugar.

Steeping guide
Tea leaves **3 g** Water amount **250 ml** Water temperature **Boiling**
Steeping time **About 4 minutes**

BALANCE

Umami · Aroma · Sweetness · Bitterness · Astringency · Acidity

Goishicha 碁石茶

Due to its rather odd appearance, it can be hard to believe that this is tea, but this fermented rarity has been produced in Kochi prefecture on the island of Shikoku for generations. After steaming, the leaves are stacked and left to mold for 7–10 days, then packed in a barrel where they are fermented with lactobacillus. After two weeks, the tea is taken out, cut into small blocks and dried in the sun. The result is a tea unlike most others, with a prominent sourness and dark liquor. In the past, goishicha was used as an ingredient in rice porridge but currently is treasured as a rare tea, drunk pure without any additives to fully enjoy its originality. Apart from goishicha produced on the island of Shikoku, similar teas, such as ishizuchi san kurocha from Ehime prefecture and awabancha from Tokushima prefecture, are also cultivated. They are only produced in small quantities and it is very rare to come across them these days.

Steeping guide
Tea leaves **2 g** Water amount **200 ml** Water temperature **Boiling**
Steeping time **1 minute**

Chapter Two

What Gives Japanese Teas Their Distinctive Flavors?

After the dormancy of winter, tea plants resprout in spring and new soft buds rich in nutrition come to life. These young buds will grow and eventually turn into ichibancha, the first harvest of the year.

Since the young buds are very sensitive to cold, the farmers take great care to protect them from frost or weather related effects as they mature. When up to five new leaves have been produced, the plant is ready for harvesting. Usually the bud is picked together with the two or sometimes three leaves on the side. In Japan, it is common to use different types of mechanical harvesters but the best quality teas are picked by hand. The plucked leaves are kept in a cool, dark place to prevent any withering and steamed as soon as there are enough leaves for a single batch.

There is no withering process for Japanese green teas, which differentiates them from other types of teas. As a result, the natural flavors remain intact as the leaves are prepared for the next stage. First, they are rattled in order to get rid of any surface moisture. When the surface dries, pressure is added to extract the moisture from the inner part of the leaves. To turn the leaves into a dry product without crushing them is a fundamental part of tea making. It takes about five hours from steaming until the finished aracha is produced, and since the condition of the leaves changes fast

"The Various Stages of Processing Japanese Sencha (Aracha)"

Fresh leaves ······> After steaming ······> After rattling the leaves ······> After primary/ rough rolling

the producer has to make several critical decisions within a short period.

Tea is not rolled directly by hand or by machine. Instead, the leaves are rolled against one another. In order to dry the leaves evenly, it is important to pick those that are of similar shape and size. In other words, high-quality tea requires great care is taken at the plantation as the tea must be carefully plucked. Before the final drying process, the leaves go through a fine rolling stage where they are stretched out into their characteristic needle-like shape. Stems and leaves originally differ in shape, but since steaming makes the leaves soft and malleable they eventually end up looking the same as they are rolled and dried together. Coming from a camellia, the tea leaf has a glossy side, which tends to make up the surface of the dried leaves when two

or three leaves and a bud are picked carefully. This is the reason why high-quality Japanese teas tend to have the deep green color and glossy leaves reminiscent of a precious stone.

After rolling/ ·····> After ·····> After fine rolling ·····> After drying
kneading intermediary
rolling

The Importance of Tea Refining in Japan

In order to understand the world of Japanese tea, it is crucial to know what tea refining is and how it is carried out in Japan as opposed to other tea producing countries. Japanese tea farmers produce something called *aracha* 荒茶, often translated as "raw tea" or "unrefined tea," which still contains a large amount of stems and dust-like leaf particles that are a result of the manufacturing process. At this stage, the tea is still considered a raw material rather than a final product. Fannings (tea dust), stems and leaves that can cause a harsh taste are sifted out. Any twigs,

stones or other foreign objects are also removed. Another important step is to reduce the moisture level. Aracha still has about 5 percent moisture, whereas refined tea (*shiagecha* 仕上げ茶) has 3 percent or less. This drying process is called *hiire* 火入れ in Japanese (written with the Chinese characters for "fire" and "enter," often translated as "firing" or "finish firing"). Reducing the moisture content enhances both the aroma and taste. Tea refining in Japan is mainly carried out by wholesalers. In order to maintain a high quality, this step is indispensable.

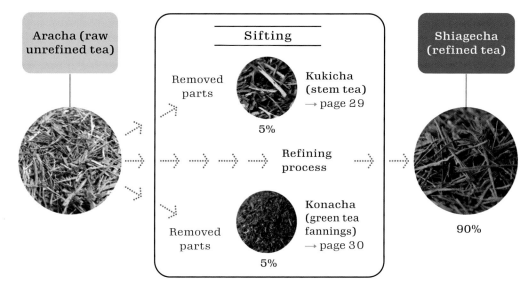

Aracha (raw unrefined tea)

Sifting

Removed parts

Kukicha (stem tea) → page 29

5%

Refining process

Konacha (green tea fannings) → page 30

Removed parts

5%

Shiagecha (refined tea)

90%

The refining process is crucial as it turns tea into a storable dry product with a stable shelf life.

Involving everything from sifting to firing, the process requires both skill and special equipment and is usually carried out by a professional tea refiner.

Handrolled Teas

Almost all teas in Japan are mechanically processed. Handrolled tea is mainly made by tea producers in order to pass on the traditional craft rather than for commercial purposes. Making handmade sencha is extremely labor intensive and requires physical strength, mental persistence, a great deal of skill and many years of experience. As with tea that is processed mechanically, at first the moisture of the surface is removed by rattling the leaves.

Then, pressure is added and the leaves are rolled and kneaded against one another to extract the moisture within. This is done on a wooden work table called a *hoiro* covered with *washi*, traditional Japanese paper. The hoiro's surface was traditionally heated from below with charcoal but now a gas burner is more commonly used. It takes five hours of labor for a skilled tea master to transform about 4.5 pounds (2 kg) of leaves into less than 1 pound (400 g) of finished tea. One can imagine how hard producers must have worked in the past before tea processing became mechanized.

Blending

"Shizuoka for the color, Kyoto for the aroma and Sayama for the taste." This is a common phrase long used in the tea industry to promote tea from Sayama. The descriptions are, of course, simplifications and the characteristics of the regions mentioned above are not entirely true. Nonetheless, the adage expresses how Japanese tea is seen as something that is blended (*gogumi*), a practice that has dominated the industry ever since modernization was introduced. The reason for this can be found in the history of tea distribution. In Japan, a producer does not make the final product but something called *aracha* (see page 40) that wholesalers, who have the refining equipment, then turn into a finished tea. However, as the wholesalers purchase aracha from many different producers, they not only refine the tea but also blend it to even out the quality and flavor and to stabilize the price. From the perspective of a producer, blending causes the tea to lose its personal signature

and character. On the other hand, tea refiners each have their own style, which gives the tea its unique characteristics. Wholesalers/refiners are concentrated in Uji and Shizuoka, two regions that apart from being tea growing areas also act as major refining and distribution centers where most Japanese tea passes through before ending up on the shelves of tea shops and stores.

Selecting teas for a blend and figuring out the proportions are usually the tasks of a skilled blender with many years of experience in the field. Once the recipe is decided upon, the teas are mixed in a blending machine.

Evaluating the Quality of Japanese Teas

Many people probably imagine that tea evaluation or grading is about being able to distinguish the difference between tea from a number of regions, producers and cultivars. The main reason for quality evaluation, however, is to detect any defects and to determine the value of tea. Examples of defects are unwanted flavors and harsh tastes that appear either during cultivation or processing. Smokiness, an oily odor or the smell from remaining pesticides are some of the problems to look out for. Tea is also checked for any manufacturing fault. This type of tea evaluation is mainly carried out by wholesalers/refiners so that a flawed product does not appear on the market. The assessment process also gives the producers feedback on their tea based on objective evaluations. Any defects or problems are reported and this information helps the producers improve their processing skills.

To evaluate Japanese tea, small white porcelain bowls are used, making it easier to assess the color of both the infused leaves and the liquor. Three grams of aracha are used, and to make any flaws or defects as easily perceived as possible

boiling water is added. A flat mesh strainer is used for assessing the aroma of the infused leaves and a teaspoon is used for tasting the tea liquor. Not only is the quality checked but the taster also takes notes on its characteristics and possible ways of refining and blending it.

LEFT The purpose of tea evaluation is to gather as much information as possible about the samples. Boiling water enables both flaws and positive characteristics to be easily detected.

ABOVE When evaluating the aroma, a strainer spoon is used to lift the wet leaves from the evaluation bowl. The spoon is tilted so that the vapors from the tea enter the nostrils, not engulf the whole face.

Chapter Three

Single Estate
Japanese Teas

What are Single Estate Japanese Teas?

Although almost all Japanese teas are blends, single estate Japanese teas are now receiving more attention. As the name implies, single estate Japanese tea is made from tea leaves picked from one tea garden, processed into aracha and then refined without blending. As with single vineyard wine, drinking single estate teas allows the taste and flavor peculiar to a chosen cultivar (clone) or terroir (a region's soil, climate and terrain) to be enjoyed. Cultivars were introduced on a large scale after World War II but the single estate movement gained momentum only at the beginning of the 21st century. Here, some of the cultivars that are representative of Japan are explored.

Lineages of Selected Japanese Tea Cultivars

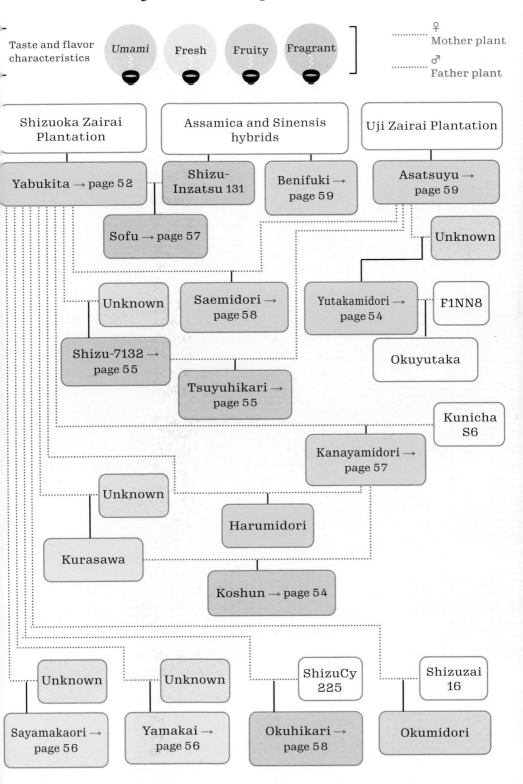

Taste and flavor characteristics

Umami Fresh Fruity Fragrant

♀ Mother plant
♂ Father plant

Shizuoka Zairai Plantation

Assamica and Sinensis hybrids

Uji Zairai Plantation

Yabukita → page 52

Shizu-Inzatsu 131

Benifuki → page 59

Asatsuyu → page 59

Sofu → page 57

Unknown

Unknown

Saemidori → page 58

Yutakamidori → page 54

F1NN8

Shizu-7132 → page 55

Okuyutaka

Tsuyuhikari → page 55

Kunicha S6

Kanayamidori → page 57

Unknown

Harumidori

Kurasawa

Koshun → page 54

Unknown

Unknown

ShizuCy 225

Shizuzai 16

Sayamakaori → page 56

Yamakai → page 56

Okuhikari → page 58

Okumidori

Zairai (在来種) Seed-Propagated Tea Gardens

The tea plant does not self-pollinate, thus cultivars are all clones propagated by cuttings. As such, they grow almost evenly into perfect hedges. On the other hand, in a so-called zairai tea garden, all the plants are propagated by seeds that are the result of natural cross-pollination. Individual plants grow at a different pace and the color and shape of the leaves also vary. Each plant has not only its own appearance but its own distinct taste and flavor, making zairai tea something of a natural blend. The taste and aroma are not as clear and refined as single cultivar teas, but if hints of wilderness or nature can be sensed in green tea, in general this attribute is undoubtedly most strongly accentuated in zairai tea. Before the introduction of clonal cultivars, all tea plants used to be propagated this way, but now zairai comprise only about 2 percent of all tea gardens in Japan. Zairai is often translated as "Japanese native," which is misleading since tea is not native to Japan but thought to have been brought from China by Buddhist monks.

OPPOSITE *A zairai (naturally cross-pollinated tea) plantation in Kasuga, Gifu prefecture.*

TOP **Detail of a zairai estate where tea plants have been propagated by seeds.**

BOTTOM **Detail of a cultivar (cloned tea plant) propagated from cuttings.**

Umami

The Yabukita Cultivar やぶきた

Yabukita is, without a doubt, the cultivar that has the best balance of the four taste elements that make up Japanese tea: *umami*, sweetness, astringency and bitterness. It also has a beautiful appearance. Good-quality yabukita will produce a sweet aroma that conjures thoughts of Japan's mist-clad mountainous regions. It was singled out from a zairai plantation in Shizuoka prefecture by Hikosaburo Sugiyama in 1908. As yabukita covers a total of about 70 percent of all the tea gardens in Japan,

it can be said to serve as a standard for Japanese tea. Depending on the region and processing method, the taste and flavor will be different. By trying various yabukita teas, the depth of this truly unique cultivar becomes apparent.

*Shizuoka Prefecture Tea Research Center / 1953
Selected by Hikosaburo Sugiyama in 1908

*Institution and registration year

The Tsukijitobetto Tea Garden 築地東頭

Half a mile (800 m) above sea level, deep in the mountains of Shizuoka prefecture, lies a stunningly beautiful tea garden that can only be reached on foot. Because of the area's harsh environment, with steep slopes and dips in temperature, tea is picked only once a year and carefully by hand. The cultivar grown is yabukita. Due to its peculiar environment, the tea has a deep aroma that is found there and nowhere else. In pursuit of the ideal sencha, Katsumi Tsukiji, who cleared and cultivated this area called Tobetto, managed to create a wonderful example of a single estate Japanese tea.

Fragrant

Umami

Koshun 香駿

Close your eyes while sipping on a koshun sencha and you might think you are standing amidst a garden in full bloom. More and more tea drinkers are charmed by this floral aroma. Koshun also has a pleasant aftertaste that lasts for a surprisingly long time. The fruity notes are balanced by a comparably strong bitterness. In the world of beer, you would find the equivalent in an IPA.

Shizuoka Prefecture Tea Research Center / 2000

Yutakamidori ゆたかみどり

After yabukita, yutakamidori covers the second largest area of all Japanese cultivars. Although bred in Shizuoka, most of it is grown in Kagoshima prefecture. It has a slightly strong bitterness, but since most of it is processed into fukamushi sencha, yutakamidori teas tend to have a mild and smooth taste with a sweetness reminiscent of root vegetables.

National Institute of Fruit Tree and Tea Science, Kanaya Japan / 1966

Fragrant

Fragrant

Tsuyuhikari つゆひかり

Tsuyuhikari is a crossbreed between shizu-7132 and asatusyu. The former has notes of cherry blossom whereas the latter has more prominent vegetal notes. Apart from a good balance between the attribute of its parents, tsuyuhikari is also comparably sweet and is therefore treasured as a tea that can be drunk by people who prefer mild teas.

Shizuoka Prefecture Tea Research Center / 2003

Shizu-7132 静-7132

The Japanese spring is famous for its cherry blossoms, or sakura in Japanese. Having an aroma resembling sakura without any added flavoring, this wonderful cultivar always offers a delightful reminder of the beauty of Japanese spring regardless of where or when it is enjoyed. As the plant was never registered, it never got a proper name but still goes by the number it was given at the research stage.

Shizuoka Prefecture Tea Research Center (never registered)

Fruity

Fresh

Yamakai 山峡

To bring out the *umami* and melon notes that are particular to this rare cultivar, steep a thick, rich infusion using iced water and a large amount of leaves. Due to its rich taste, it also goes by the nickname "natural gyokuro," but unlike gyokuro high-quality yamakai can also be steeped in hot water.

Shizuoka Prefecture Tea Research Center / 1967

Sayamakaori さやまかおり

The way the leaves grow evenly almost like needles at the plantation gives this cultivar its unique look. Comparatively weak in *umami*, it has a mouthfeel that could be described as light-bodied, while the refreshing astringency and forest-like aroma invigorate the mind. The characteristic sweetness makes this cultivar stand out.

Saitama Prefecture Tea Research Center / 1971

Fruity

Fruity

Kanayamidori かなやみどり

This cultivar is known for having a milky flavor, but depending on the growing conditions and processing method it changes considerably, sometimes having fruity notes resembling citrus. If drunk when winter turns into spring, it conjures the rejuvenation of spring.

National Institute of Fruit Tree and Tea Science, Kanaya Japan / 1970

Sofu 蒼風

Unique muscatel notes, perhaps a result of its partly Indian genome and flowery aroma, are the main characteristics of this cultivar, which also has typical Japanese attributes such as strong *umami*. It tastes good even when steeped like black tea, in hot water, with slightly fewer leaves.

National Institute of Fruit Tree and Tea Science, Kanaya Japan / 2002

Fragrant

Umami

Okuhikari おくひかり

A little stronger than yabukita and with
a sweet aroma, this cultivar displays
both steadiness and persistence in taste
as well as flavor. As such, it is cherished
by many devoted green tea drinkers.
Although it lacks grandiosity, it has a
subtle beauty, making it a gustatory
expression of the Japanese aesthetic
ideal: wabi sabi.

Shizuoka Prefecture Tea Research Center / 1987

Saemidori さえみどり

In a sense, saemidori is similar to
yabukita but with less bitterness and
astringency. It makes a good first green
tea for beginners. This cultivar, which
is enjoyed mainly for its sweetness and
umami, does not become too bitter even
when exposed to strong sunlight, which
is one reason for its popularity in flat
tea growing regions like Kagoshima.

**National Institute of Fruit Tree and Tea Science,
Makurazaki Japan / 1990**

Fresh

Fruity

Asatsuyu あさつゆ

This cultivar was selected from an Uji zairai plantation. Its prominent vegetal notes resembling green vegetables give it a distinct "green" impression. If yabukita has a sharpness to it, the mouthfeel of asatsuyu can be said to be more rounded and smooth.

National Institute of Fruit Tree and Tea Science, Kanaya Japan / 1953

Benifuki べにふうき

Benifuki was originally bred as a black tea cultivar and it certainly has typical black tea attributes such as astringency and a peach-like fruitiness. When made into green tea, the astringency becomes very prominent while the methylated catechin, which is reported to ease hay fever symptoms, goes unchanged, one reason why it is also consumed as a green tea.

National Institute of Fruit Tree and Tea Science, Makurazaki Japan / 1993

Chapter Four

Japan's Main
Tea Growing Regions

Japan's Main Tea Growing Regions

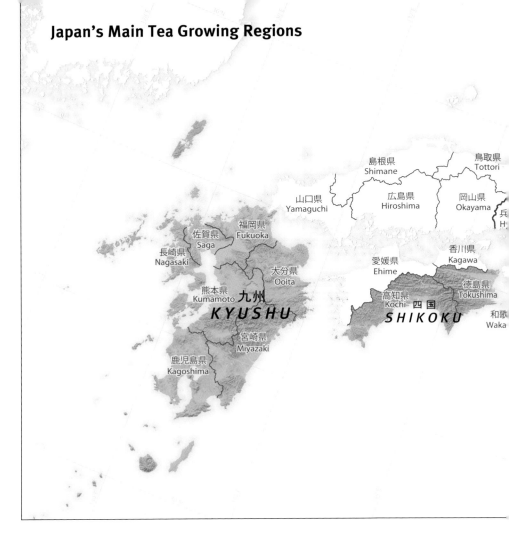

島根県
Shimane

鳥取県
Tottori

山口県
Yamaguchi

広島県
Hiroshima

岡山県
Okayama

兵
H

福岡県
Fukuoka

佐賀県
Saga

長崎県
Nagasaki

大分県
Ooita

熊本県
Kumamoto

九州
KYUSHU

宮崎県
Miyazaki

鹿児島県
Kagoshima

愛媛県
Ehime

香川県
Kagawa

高知県
Kochi 四国

徳島県
Tokushima

SHIKOKU

和歌
Waka

A Brief Timeline for Japanese Tea

805 The Buddhist monk Saicho returns from Tang China and is said to have planted tea at the foot of Mount Hie near Kyoto.

815 The Buddhist monk Eichu offered tea to the Saga emperor.

1191 The Buddhist monk Yosai (Eisai) is thought to have planted tea seeds at Sefuriyama in Kyushu.

1207 The Buddhist monk Myoe is said to have planted the tea seeds he received from Yosai at Togano Kozanji near Kyoto.

1211 Yosai completes the first literary work on tea in Japan, *Kissa Yojoki*.

1236
1573 During the Muromachi era, the Japanese tea ceremony takes form.

1610 The Dutch East India Company imports Japanese tea for the first time.

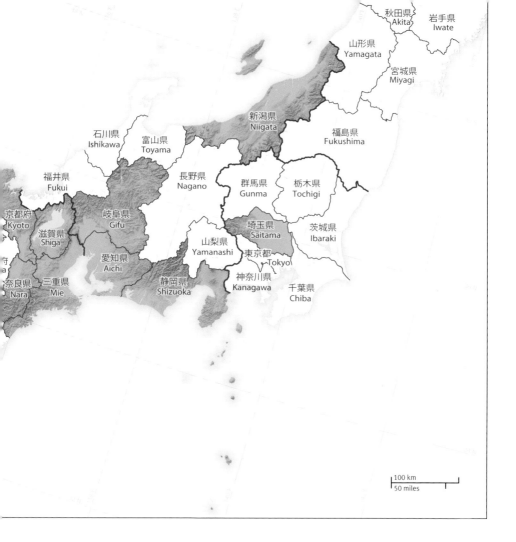

1738   Nagatani Soen develops the processing method for sencha in Uji.

1835   Kahei Yamamoto invents gyokuro.

1858   The Treaty of Amenity and Commerce between the United States and the Empire of Japan is signed. Tea exports gain momentum.

1869   The Makinohara plateau in Shizuoka is cleared by former samurai and tea cultivation starts. Exports soar.

1906   Kakuzo Okakura's famous work, *The Book of Tea*, is published in the United States.

1908   The Yabukita cultivar is singled out by Hikosaburo Sugiyama.

1960s   During the 1960s and beyond, the production method for fukamushi sencha is developed. The introduction of cultivars advances rapidly.

1985   Canned green tea is sold for the first time.

Japan's Main Tea Growing Areas

Tea is grown from Okinawa in the south to the Hokuriku area in the northwest of Honshu, but most production is concentrated in central Japan, the Kansai area and the island of Kyushu. The different regions have their specific tastes and flavors. In many cases, different tea types are produced, with some specializing in sencha, others producing gyokuro, kabusecha and even Chinese-style pan-fired tea. Two regions, Kyoto and Shizuoka, stand out for being not only tea producing areas but also distribution centers where tea from many other regions is refined and blended. In modern Japan, sencha is often taken for granted, with many people tending to believe that it has been consumed in the same way for hundreds of years. The history of sencha, however, is much shorter than many other types of tea. It became a common beverage only after World War II. Before then, most tea consumed in Japan was of a different color, shape and taste.

Characteristics of tea grown in flat regions

Mainly fukamushi sencha
Deep green liquor
Rich, round taste
Smooth mouthfeel

Characteristics of tea grown in mountainous regions

Mainly sencha
Bright golden yellow liquor
Balanced taste and strong aroma
Slightly astringent

Nagatani Soen's dwelling

Both the habit of drinking tea and the plant itself are believed to have been introduced from China. Japanese monks played the main role in bringing back different kinds of Chinese tea, depending on the era in which they happened to live. From the Tang dynasty they imported the tradition of cooking and boiling a type of pressed tea, from the Song dynasty came powdered tea and, finally, from the Ming dynasty came the habit of using teapots to steep tea and drink the resulting infusion. Gradually, not only the tea itself but also its cultivation and production took hold in Japan.

Tea masters like Sen No Rikyu shaped the Japanese tea ceremony from the 16th century onward, turning the powdered tea matcha into something truly Japanese both in terms of cultivation and processing. As for Senchado, or the "Way of Sencha," which was formed in the 18th century during the middle of the Edo period, the influence from China remains strong even today, especially in the teaware used.

The processing method for sencha, or at least the base for it, was developed in 1738, an achievement credited to Nagatani Soen from Ujitawara in modern-day Kyoto prefecture. The new tea was steamed after plucking, then dried while rolled and kneaded, the taste and flavor dissolving easily even when steeped in a teapot. However, tea that was cooked and boiled to make an extract retained its position as a mainstream beverage, and it was not until after World War II that sencha secured its position as the typical tea consumed by most Japanese. This was how a truly Japanese leaf tea was finally born. Much has happened since then and it keeps evolving, with new types appearing every year.

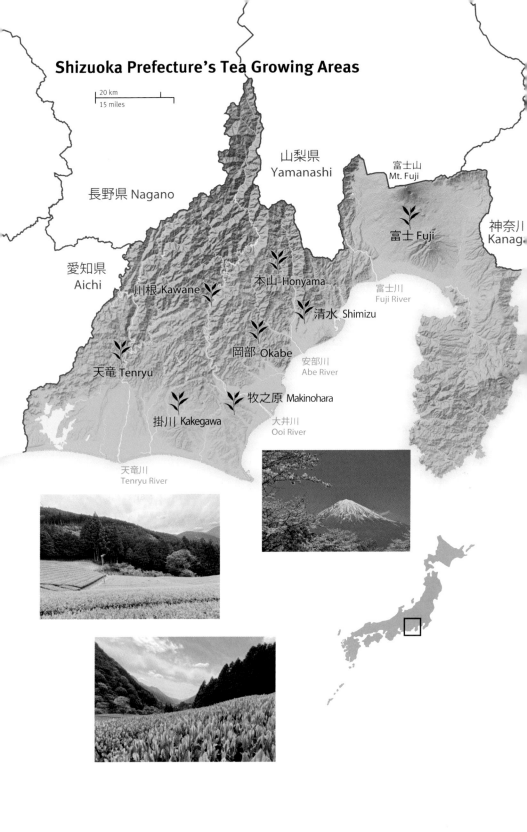

Shizuoka Prefecture's Tea Growing Areas

20 km
15 miles

長野県 Nagano

山梨県 Yamanashi

富士山 Mt. Fuji

愛知県 Aichi

神奈川 Kanag

本山 Honyama

川根 Kawane

富士 Fuji

清水 Shimizu

富士川 Fuji River

岡部 Okabe

天竜 Tenryu

安部川 Abe River

牧之原 Makinohara

掛川 Kakegawa

大井川 Ooi River

天竜川 Tenryu River

Shizuoka Prefecture

Shizuoka has long been synonymous with green tea production. Famous for Mount Fuji, the region has the ideal climate for tea cultivation, giving rise to some of the world's finest sencha. Even when seen from the shinkansen bullet train, it is easy to tell that this is a full-fledged tea region as you look out over the beautiful green scenery of the tea gardens. The tea often gets labeled "Shizuoka tea," but Shizuoka stretches far from east to west, with altitudes ranging from high to low, so the teas from the respective sub-regions have their own distinct tastes and flavors. The yield can be roughly divided into sato no ocha (literally "tea from the village"), which is grown in flat areas, and yama no ocha ("mountain tea"), which is, as the term suggests, grown in high-altitude regions. Not only the environment but also the processing methods differ. Comparably flat areas like Makinohara and Kakegawa mainly produce fukamushi sencha, whereas sencha is the most common type of tea in mountainous regions like Shizuoka City, Shimada and Hamamatsu. Shizuoka further displays its great variety as mass production and single estate tea are found in the same prefecture. Further-more, Shizuoka is not only a tea produc-ing region but, like Kyoto, an area where tea is refined and blended. Tea refiners and wholesalers are concentrated in large numbers, and as tea from other regions is traded and refined in large quantities, Shizuoka also serves as a large distribution center for Japanese tea. In addition, yabukita and many other cultivars that are grown all over Japan have their origin in Shizuoka. In the prefecture, yabukita covers about 90 percent of all tea gardens, but since the total production volume is so great, considerable quantities of other culti-vars, such as okuhikari, yamakai and koshun, are also grown.

Honyama

The tea growing region along the upper branch of the Abe River is commonly referred to as Honyama, and it produces

an excellent example of mountain tea. The color of the liquor is golden yellow and it has a pleasant astringency. The aftertaste lingers for a long time and this, together with the sweet aroma that you can only get from mountain teas, is characteristic of Honyama tea. Since many of the tea gardens are located on steep slopes, the terrain is not especially suited for agriculture, making this area unfit for mass production. Instead, tea from this region is valued for its quality. The history is long, stretching back as far as the Kamakura period (1185–1333) when Shoichi Kokushi, a Buddhist monk, brought tea seeds back from China and planted them in Shizuoka, purportedly in the village of Ashikubo, which is part of the Honyama area.

Main cultivars: Yabukita, Okuhikari, Yamakai

Makinohara

The first thing that strikes a visitor to the Makinohara plateau are the vast tea gardens stretching almost as far as the eye can see. Yet, despite the expansive fields Makinohara has a relatively short history as a tea growing region. During the Meiji Restoration in the late 1800s, the samurai lost their privileges. At the same time, the construction of bridges over Japan's many rivers made ferrymen and river transport workers unnecessary. These workers joined forces with the samurai to clear part of the land that made up the Makinohara plateau, thus paving the way for new occupations as tea farmers. Tea export took off during the last years of the Tokugawa shogunate. The hope of increased revenues from trade with foreign countries was the main motivating factor for those who established tea estates in the area. Currently, most of the tea produced in Makinohara is consumed in Japan but in the beginning almost all of it was shipped to the largest importer of Japanese tea at the time, the United States. The main cultivar is yabukita and the tea produced is essentially fukamushi sencha. However, attempts to diversify cultivation are being made, with the cultivar tsuyuhikari being grown to a larger degree in recent years.

Main cultivar: Yabukita

Kawane

Tea from Kawane, together with Hon-yama tea, is usually referred to as mountain tea. The tea leaves are picked when they are still soft and tender, and they tend to resemble the sencha curled into fine needles that is often seen at official tea competitions. The most common cultivar is yabukita but the slightly stronger okuhikari, which has a notable sweet fragrance, is also grown in the region.

Main cultivars: Yabukita, Okuhikari

Kakegawa

Tea is not only produced but also consumed in large quantities in Kakegawa, an area that has received much attention for its residents' long life expectancy. Since tea drinking is thought to be one of the possible contributing factors to longevity, this has made Kakegawa tea well-known throughout Japan. It belongs to the category of village teas. Mainly fukamushi sencha from Yabukita is produced, often with a slightly stronger aroma compared to other regions that produce similar teas.

Main cultivar: Yabukita

Shizuoka: Other Regions

Tea is grown throughout almost the entire Shizuoka region. Shimizu and Tenryu are examples of mountain teas, whereas Kikugawa and Fukuroi belong to the village tea group. Most subregions produce either sencha or fukamushi sencha, but Okabe stands out as a gyokuro producing area. The Fuji area is also noted for its picturesque tea gardens stretching out to the foot of Mount Fuji.

Kansai's Tea Growing Areas

50 km
20 miles

福井県 Fukui
滋賀県 Shiga
岐阜県 Gifu

琵琶湖 Lake Biwa

京都府 Kyoto
宇治田原 Ujitawara
京田辺 Kyotanabe
和束 Wazuka
南山城 Minamiyamashiro
KYOTO

滋賀 Shiga

政所 Mandokoro
朝宮 Asamiya

水沢 Suizawa
鈴鹿 Suzuka
亀山 Kameyama

愛知県 Aichi

兵庫県 Hyogo

宇治 Uji

三重 Mie

伊勢茶 Isecha

OSAKA

月ヶ瀬 Tsukigase

大和茶 Yamatocha

飯南 Iinan
飯高 Iitaka
度会 Watarai

大阪府 Osaka

奈良 Nara

三重県 Mie

和歌山県 Wakayama

奈良県 Nara

70

The Kansai Region

Kyoto Prefecture

Kyoto produces more tencha (the raw material for matcha) than any other prefecture but it is also the originator of both sencha and gyokuro. Not only a region of cultivation, tea from other places is refined and blended in Kyoto, thereby making it one of the main centers for tea distribution in Japan.

Compared to Shizuoka and Kagoshima, the production volume is rather small but many different kinds of tea are produced, with a wide variety of cultivars grown. In particular, the art of shading tea plants is a highly developed and common practice in Kyoto, and its tencha and gyokuro are praised as teas of the highest quality. Special cultivars for this purpose, such as asahi, samidori, goko and ujihikari, all have their origin in Kyoto.

In the Tokai area and in Kyushu, fukamushi sencha is common but in Kyoto and the rest of the Kansai area it is almost nonexistent.

As a tea growing region, Kyoto has a long history stretching back to when Myoe, a monk at Togano Kozan temple, received tea seeds from Yosai (also called Eisai), another monk who brought them back from Song dynasty China in 1191. In the 14th century, when tea tasting games were a popular pastime among the warrior class, Togano tea was seen as the true tea, while all the rest were lumped together as "non-teas."

Uji

Uji is probably the most widely known regional tea brand from Japan but it actually consists of a blend of tea from four prefectures: Kyoto and neighboring Shiga, Nara and Mie. Tea production in Uji proper is dominated by tencha and gyokuro, with their intense *umami* and a seaweed-like aroma. Traditionally, the tea gardens were shaded with a reed screen and straw, but that practice is increasingly rare as most farmers now use a black synthetic cloth instead.

Main cultivars: Samidori, Goko, Asahi

Other Regions in Kyoto

Kyoto is famous for Uji tea but the largest tea producing area in the prefecture is Wazuka. Kyotababe is an area famous for gyokuro. Other tea growing areas are Minamiyamashiro, Joyo, Yawata and Ujitawara. Although located in the same prefecture, many different teas are produced, both shaded and non-shaded. In recent years, more producers in these regions are attempting to sell their tea as single estate teas rather than letting them be blended into ujicha.

Main cultivars: Yabukita, Okumidori, Zairai

Shiga Prefecture

According to legend, Saicho, a monk returning from Tang dynasty China in 805, planted tea seeds at the foot of Mount Hie. The small Hiyoshi tea garden found in Otsu in Shiga prefecture may be the remains of this site. Most of the tea produced in Shiga is transported to Uji for blending, but some of the teas from subregions like Asamiya and Mandokoro are also sold as single estate teas. Mandokoro, where many old zairai plantations can be found, is highly valued as a producer of rare teas.

Main cultivars: Yabukita, Zairai

Nara Prefecture

Nara produces mainly kabusecha, a type of tea that, with its sweet taste and distinct seaweed-like aroma, is popular both in Kyoto and the Kansai region as a whole. As with other teas grown in Kansai, most Nara tea also gets blended in Uji but some of it is sold under the brand name "Yamato-cha," or even as single estate tea from subregions like Tsukigase.

Main cultivars: Yabukita, Okumidori, Zairai

Mie Prefecture

Mie is Japan's third largest tea producer after Shizuoka and Kagoshima, but since most of the tea gets blended in Kyoto as ujicha, one is unlikely to come across pure Mie tea. Kabuse-cha is the most common type. During the harvest season, the lush green hedges of the tea farms are completely covered by the synthetic black cloth commonly used. Some of the tea produced in Mie is sold as "Isecha." Mie is not only a tea growing region but is also famous for Yokkaichi's Banko teapots.

Main cultivars: Yabukita, Zairai

Tea Regions in Central and Eastern Japan

Despite being on a smaller scale compared to the largest tea growing regions, many famous tea areas are located in central and eastern Japan on the main island of Honshu. North of Tokyo is Saitama, also known as Sayama in the context of tea. Further north in the same direction is the border line of tea cultivation, shared by Niigata on the west coast and and Ibaraki on the east coast. In Central Japan, Aichi is famous for nishio matcha and for Tokoname teaware. North of Aichi is Gifu, a mountainous region mostly known for shirakawa tea.

Sayama

The regional brand name "Sayama" includes all tea made in Saitama prefecture. Although small, it is one of the oldest tea growing regions in Japan. Its origin is unclear, but the earliest reliable records, which date back to the Nanboku era (1336–1392), mention Musashi Kawagoe in Saitama as a tea growing region. Today, fukamushi sencha, made from yabukita, is the most common type of tea produced.

Main cultivars: Yabukita, Sayamakaori, Fukumidori

Nishio

Nishio in Aichi prefecture almost exclusively produces tencha, and after Kyoto boasts the country's second largest production volume. Just like in neighboring Shizuoka, the monk Shoichi Kokushi is usually credited with introducing tea to Aichi prefecture during the Kamakura era. However, it would take until the Meiji era, when tea making skills were introduced from Kyoto, for tea production to really take off in Nishio.

Main cultivars: Yabukita, Samidori

Gifu

Ibi and Shirakawa are two subregions of Gifu, and their snow-covered tea gardens in winter reveal how much colder it is there than in most other tea regions of Japan. Kasuga along the Ibi River is a rare sight, as many old zairai plantations remain. In the Shirakawa area, yabukita is the most commonly grown cultivar. The tea has a slightly broken appearance that when steeped gives the liquor a rich green color.

Main cultivars: Yabukita, Okumidori, Zairai

Other Regions in Eastern Japan

There are many regions in Japan that produce tea on a small scale but the line between Murakami in Niigata prefecture and Daigo in Ibaraki prefecture is considered to be the northern limit for commercial tea farming in Japan. Tea is also grown in Kanagawa and Chiba prefectures but in limited quantities.

Central and Eastern Japan's Tea Growing Areas

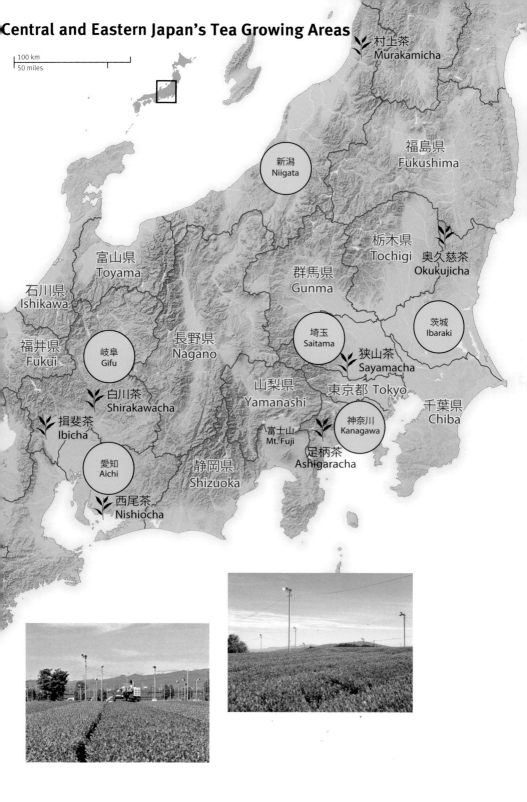

100 km
50 miles

村上茶
Murakamicha

福島県
Fukushima

新潟
Niigata

栃木県
Tochigi

奥久慈茶
Okukujicha

群馬県
Gunma

富山県
Toyama

茨城
Ibaraki

石川県
Ishikawa

長野県
Nagano

埼玉
Saitama

狭山茶
Sayamacha

福井県
Fukui

岐阜
Gifu

東京都 Tokyo

山梨県
Yamanashi

千葉県
Chiba

白川茶
Shirakawacha

神奈川
Kanagawa

揖斐茶
Ibicha

富士山
Mt. Fuji

足柄茶
Ashigaracha

愛知
Aichi

静岡県
Shizuoka

西尾茶
Nishiocha

Kyushu and Shikoku in Southern Japan

Shikoku Island

The island of Shikoku only produces small quantities of tea compared to other regions but it is famous as the home of teas fermented by micro-organisms, a rarity in Japan. Examples are teas like goishicha (see page 35) from Kochi, awabancha from Tokushima and ishizuchi san kurocha from Ehime. They are very different from typical Japanese tea, having a strong sourness and a particular earthy taste.

Fukuoka Prefecture

The oldest tea garden in Fukuoka dates to the Kamakura era when Yosai (also called Eisai) is said to have cultivated tea at Sefuri Mountain on the border of Saga prefecture. Fukuoka has a long tea tradition, earning renown for its "Yame" tea, a fukamushi sencha regional brand, and for its production of gyokuro. Apart from the cultivars grown for making gyokuro, yabukita dominates, but in recent years other cultivars like tsuyuhikari are also gaining prominence.

Main cultivars: Yabukita, Kanayamidori, Saemidori

Southern Japan's Tea Growing Areas

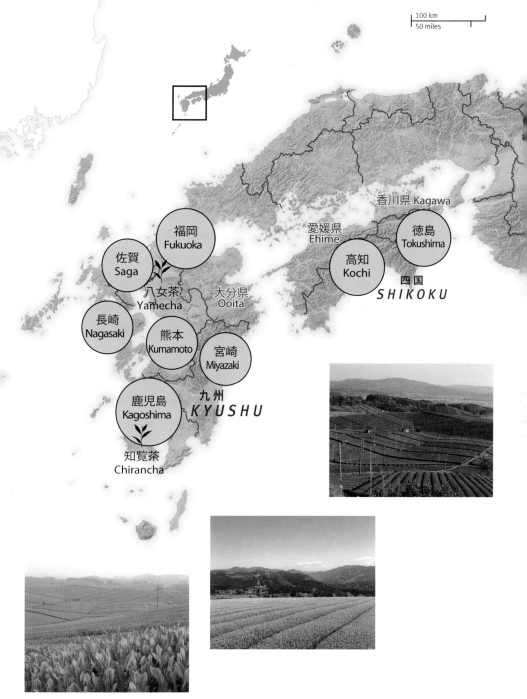

100 km
50 miles

香川県 Kagawa

愛媛県
Ehime

徳島
Tokushima

福岡
Fukuoka

佐賀
Saga

高知
Kochi

四国
SHIKOKU

八女茶
Yamecha

大分県
Ooita

長崎
Nagasaki

熊本
Kumamoto

宮崎
Miyazaki

鹿児島
Kagoshima

九州
KYUSHU

知覧茶
Chirancha

Kagoshima Prefecture

Kagoshima ranks second in the nation both in terms of cultivated area and production volume, but few know that it used to be a large-scale black tea region. However, due to mass production of black tea in countries like India and Sri Lanka, Japanese varieties could not compete on the international market. The decisive blow came with trade liberalization in the 1970s when import tariffs on black tea in Japan disappeared, pushing Japanese varieties out of the domestic market in favor of tea from other countries. During the same period, however, domestic demand for green tea rose and Kagoshima managed to switch to green tea production. The vast tea gardens stretching as far as the eye can see over large flat areas is a scene unique to Kagoshima. The climate is warmer than other tea growing regions in Japan, so *shincha* (first harvest) is harvested early, and even *yonbancha* (fourth harvest) and *shutoban* (fall and winter harvest) tea are harvested in considerable quantities. Tea grown in regions like Kagoshima, which have strong sunlight, tends to become bitter and astringent, so in order to preserve the natural sweetness of the tea the plants are often shaded. As another way to reduce bitterness, tea cultivars with a comparably mild taste, such as yutakamidori, saemidori and asatsuyu, are cultivated to a larger degree than in other regions. As a result, Kagoshima tea is smooth and sweet in

taste. Until a couple of years ago, Kagoshima tea was mainly shipped to Shizuoka for refining, but in recent years pure Kagoshima tea is being sold in larger quantities and regional brands like "Chiran Tea" are becoming increasingly known to the Japanese public. Kagoshima is also making great efforts to increase exports, and organic farming is expanding rapidly as a result.

Main cultivars: Yabukita, Yutakamidori, Saemidori, Asatsuyu

Other Regions in Kyushu

Tea is produced on the entire island of Kyushu but some regions like Takachiho in Miyazaki prefecture and Ureshino in Saga prefecture are known for Chinese-style pan-fired teas. Their refreshing smoothness and sweet, roasted aroma make them strikingly different from steamed Japanese tea.

How to Brew Japanese Tea

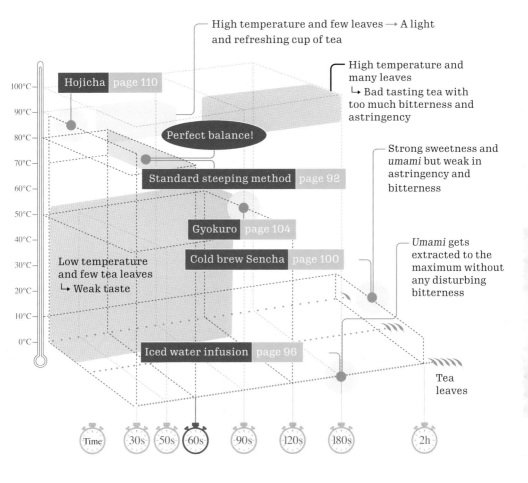

High temperature and few leaves → A light and refreshing cup of tea

High temperature and many leaves
↳ Bad tasting tea with too much bitterness and astringency

Hojicha · page 110

Perfect balance!

Standard steeping method · page 92

Strong sweetness and *umami* but weak in astringency and bitterness

Gyokuro · page 104

Cold brew Sencha · page 100

Low temperature and few tea leaves
↳ Weak taste

Umami gets extracted to the maximum without any disturbing bitterness

Iced water infusion · page 96

Tea leaves

Time · 30s · 50s · 60s · 90s · 120s · 180s · 2h

100°C · 90°C · 80°C · 70°C · 60°C · 50°C · 40°C · 30°C · 20°C · 10°C · 0°C

No other type of tea can be steeped in as many ways as steamed Japanese tea, but since it easily turns bitter it can also be difficult for the beginner. Admittedly, its components are released a lot faster than other types of tea, so it is important to pay attention to both the temperature and the steeping time. When steeping tea, there are four main factors that affect the taste: the amount of tea leaves, the amount of water, the water temperature and the steeping time. There is no correct way of steeping tea, so rather than just following a manual it is much more enjoyable to remember and then apply the logic of tea steeping to bring out the greatest variation in taste that Japanese tea has to offer.

Basic Teaware

2. Chazutsu/Chakan
Tea canister

5. Yuzamashi
Hot water cooler

1. Chasaji
Tea scoop

3. Yunomi
Teacup

4. Kyusu
Teapot

6. Futao
Lid rest

1. *Chasaji* – Tea scoop
For measuring, this is a necessity for
anyone steeping tea on a daily basis.

2. *Chazutsu/Chakan* – Tea canister
The tea canister should be as airtight as
possible. However, it is still not suitable
for storing tea over a long period so make
sure to consume it as quickly as possible.
If stored in a cool dry place, Japanese tea
can be kept in a tea canister for about a
month.

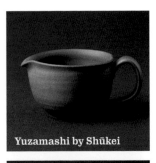

Yuzamashi by Shūkei

3. *Yunomi* – Teacup
White porcelain is good for teas steeped
after cooling down the water, such as
sencha and gyokuro. For teas drunk hot
and in large quantities, like hojicha or
bancha, thick ceramic cups are a better
choice.

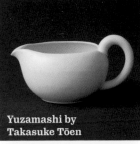

**Yuzamashi by
Takasuke Tōen**

4. *Kyusu* – Teapot
The beauty of Japanese teapots is re-
vealed on pages 114–119.

Lid rest by Teruyuki Isobe

5. *Yuzamashi* – Hot water cooler
Used for cooling down the boiled water,
the yuzamashi is an important vessel for
making Japanese tea.

6. *Futaoki* – Teapot lid rest
This is not essential but it makes it easier
to keep the teapot lid safe when not in
use.

Lid rest by Teruyuki Isobe

How to Scoop Tea

As the aim in scooping tea is to get an average sample of the tea leaves, it is important to not just take leaves from the top of the canister. Paying attention to how the tea is scooped will result in a well-balanced cup of tea. First, tilt the tea canister a little, then hold the tea scoop upside down and insert it in the upper part of the canister. Twist the canister inwards and the tea scoop outwards. The tea leaves will then fall evenly on the scoop without getting crushed or broken.

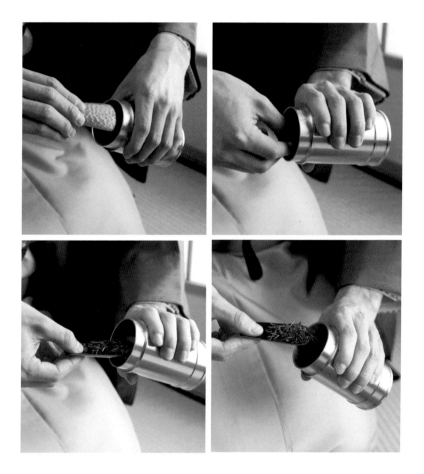

Teapot Maintenance

When you are done steeping your tea, throw away the used leaves, rinse the teapot and let it air dry. Even if the strainer gets clogged or the inside gets stained, there are easy ways to take care of a Japanese teapot. A brush can be used to clean the strainer. Light stains can be cleaned with a melamine foam sponge and tough ones by using baking soda. For teapots made of non-porous materials, oxygen-based bleach can also be used. Teas with a broken appearance like fuka-mushi sencha and konacha tend to clog the strainer so maintenance can be troublesome. For these teas, use teapots with a wide stainless strainer or a strainer basket.

How to Store Tea

When exposed to light, oxygen, moisture, heat or strong odors, the quality of tea easily degrades or alters. After opening your tea package, make sure to store the leaves in an airtight container in a dark, cool and dry place. If unopened, tea can be stored in the fridge, but make sure to let it return to room temperature before opening it to protect the leaves from condensation. For the same reason, once the package is opened, tea should never be stored in the fridge.

The Importance of Water Quality

As long as you have tea leaves, teaware and water, either hot or cold, you can enjoy Japanese tea anywhere, any time. As I crave several cups of tea a day, I never fail to take my teapot along with me whether I travel for business internationally or for leisure. During the last couple of years, I have traveled to over sixteen countries, including Japan, and have shared many precious tea moments with my small teapot from Tokoname. But even if I use the same leaves and attempt to steep under the same conditions, the taste and flavor will, of course, change at each destination because of the water. Water comprises 99.5 percent of the tea we drink, making changes in taste inevitable. So by bringing your favorite tea and teaware with you wherever you go, you are able to enjoy a relaxing tea experience, at the same time making new discoveries with something that you drink on an everyday basis.

There are many factors, including the steeping method, that affect the taste of tea, but when it comes to water, soft water, with a low level of hardness, is definitely preferable. Almost all water in Japan is soft, but when tea is steeped in an area with hard water, the *umami* will dissolve well, yet the supposedly fresh aroma becomes weak, resulting in a tea that feels heavy rather than refreshing. If you are steeping Japanese tea in an area with hard water, it is a good idea to use a water softener or to purchase bottled water that is naturally soft.

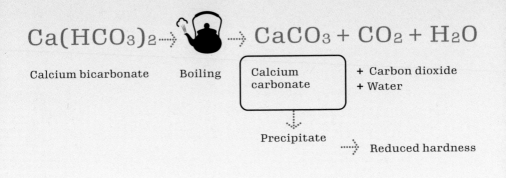

$$Ca(HCO_3)_2 \dashrightarrow \quad \dashrightarrow \quad CaCO_3 + CO_2 + H_2O$$

Calcium bicarbonate   Boiling   Calcium carbonate   + Carbon dioxide + Water

Precipitate $\dashrightarrow$ Reduced hardness

In addition to a preferred water for Japanese tea, there is also an optimal way of boiling it. Many types of green tea are thought to be steeped best at 70–80 °C (160–175 °F). However, many people seem to think that you only need to heat the water to the desired temperature without boiling it. But the water should be boiled for up to three minutes and then cooled down to the desired temperature before steeping. Although unknown even to many habitual tea drinkers, there are four reasons for boiling the water for tea. First, it helps to get rid of the smell of chlorine if there is any. Second, it releases oxygen from the water, which gives the tea a clear taste. The third reason is to sterilize the water, thus making it safer. Finally, boiling the water further reduces its hardness.

Hardness can be divided into temporary hardness and permanent hardness. In the case of temporary hardness, calcium bicarbonate (calcium hydrogen carbonate) and magnesium bicarbonate (magnesium hydrogen carbonate) are the main molecules responsible. Boiling the water promotes the formation of precipitates in the form of calcium carbonate and magnesium carbonate, carbon dioxide and water (H_2O), resulting in softer water. If you live in an area with hard or very hard water, it is particularly important not to neglect boiling your water. Permanent hardness is usually caused by calcium chloride or magnesium chloride and, unfortunately, as the name suggests, the hardness cannot be reduced by boiling.

Water quality greatly affects the taste and flavor of Japanese tea. Boiling the water before brewing is an important step as it makes the extraction of flavor more efficient.

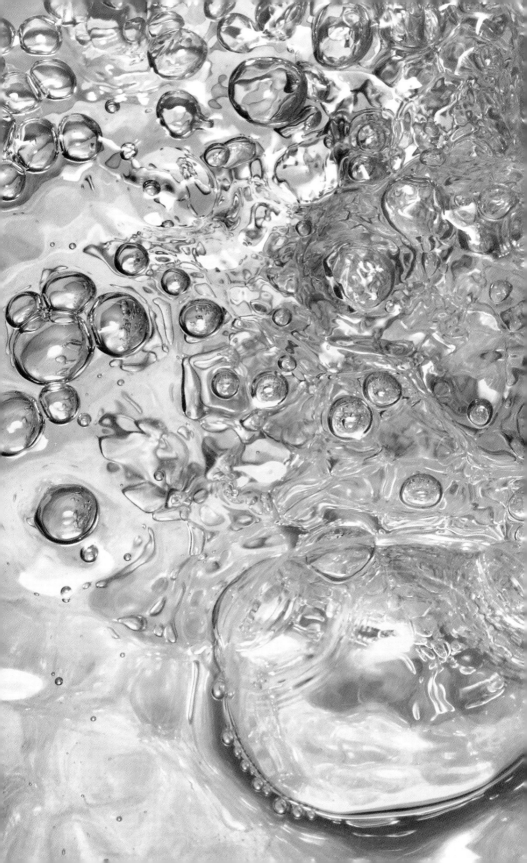

The Standard Method for Steeping Sencha

How to steep a well-balanced cup of sencha

1

First, put 6 g of sencha leaves in the teapot, the equivalent of two full Japanese tea scoops or about three teaspoons. After trying this once, increase or decrease the amount of leaves next time if the taste is not to your satisfaction.

2

Cool down the water to avoid excess bitterness, astringency and harsh flavors. By pouring boiling water from the kettle into the water cooler, the temperature drops about 10 °C. If you do not have a water cooler, any heat-resistant vessel can be used. However, a water cooler is both functional and adds to the mood, so it is definitely preferable to have one.

Other suitable teas

Fukamushi sencha (p. 21) 70 °C (160 °F) –
40 seconds

Kabusecha (p. 23) / Kukicha, Bocha (p. 29)

Kamairicha (p. 31) 80 °C (175 °F)

Steeping guide

Tea leaves **6 g**

Water **180 ml**

Water temperature **70–80 °C
(160–175 °F)**

Steeping time **1 minute**

3

In order to achieve a good balance of all
the taste elements, the water should be
cooled down to 70–80 °C (160–175 °F).
Pour hot water into the water cooler,
wait for a while and then try to hold it
carefully. At 70 °C (160 °F), most people
can bear touching it for a while but it
is still too hot to hold for a long time.
Using a thermometer a couple of times
to ascertain the temperature will help
you trust your senses next time.

4

When the water has cooled down to the
desired temperature, pour it gently into
the teapot. If the temperature is too low,
the tea will get a watery taste and the
aroma will also become weaker. To
prevent this, make sure to put on the
lid and then wait for one minute. If the
steeping time is too short, the taste
will not be fully extracted. Conversely,
steeping the tea for too long will make it
bitter and astringent.

5

Pouring energetically will result in a harsh flavor, so handle the teapot gently and pour lightly to get a cup of tea with a smooth and round flavor. If you are steeping tea for more than one person, pour the tea little by little into each cup to adjust the strength and color. Always make sure to pour to the last drop.

6

Even if all the tea is poured and no liquid remains, the teapot is still hot. This lingering heat will make the second steeping excessively bitter and much of the aroma will also be lost, so make sure to remove the teapot lid and put it on a lid rest or somewhere else safe.

How to enjoy a second steeping

Most of the *umami* comes out in the first steeping. In order to extract more of the aroma and a pleasant astringency from the second steeping, gradually raise the temperature. However, as the leaves have already opened up, steep the tea for only a few seconds before pouring it into the teacups. If you are pairing your tea with sweets, the naturally astringent second and following steepings will make a perfect match.

How to ensure even flavor intensity

When steeping tea for two or three people, it is important to pour the tea little by little into each cup to make all the cups of tea taste the same. However, this action itself will make the steeping time longer, so pouring everything into a preheated pitcher or back into the water cooler makes it easier to control the taste and flavor when steeping tea for a large number of people. Then pour the tea from the pitcher into the teacups.

Steeping Sencha in Iced Water

How to extract and indulge in a burst of *umami*

1

First, prepare ice made from soft water without any smell of chlorine to bring out the most of the tea's natural flavor. Put the ice in a small pitcher and pour cold water on top. Any vessel can be used as long as it can handle cold temperatures and has a spout. However, by using stoneware vessels you will be able to create a Japanese atmosphere. The condensation also adds a subtle beauty to the experience.

2

Put 10–15 g of sencha in the teapot. Using this much leaf when steeping tea in hot water will make it extremely bitter and astringent, but iced water will bring out only the *umami* and sweetness and turn it into an extremely rich-flavored experience.

Other suitable teas
Gyokuro (p. 22)

Steeping guide
Tea leaves **10–15 g**
Water **20 ml**
Water temperature **Iced**
Steeping time **180 seconds**

3
Use the tea scoop to spread the tea leaves evenly. Make sure to do this gently so as not to crush any of the tea leaves. A normal teapot with a small bottom will result in a heap of tea leaves with some not fully or at all immersed, so use a teapot with a flat bottom. These are called *hiragata kyusu* in Japanese.

4
Pour iced water into the pot, but only until the leaves are barely soaked. To avoid pouring too much water, pour the water a little at a time in a circular motion.

5

Steeping tea in iced water is mostly about enjoying *umami*, but preheating the small cups will make the aroma enjoyable as well. Make sure not to burn yourself when you pour hot water into the cups.

6

Pour out the hot water that is in the cups. Any remaining water droplets will weaken the tea's rich taste and give it an odd flavor, so be sure to thoroughly dry the cups.

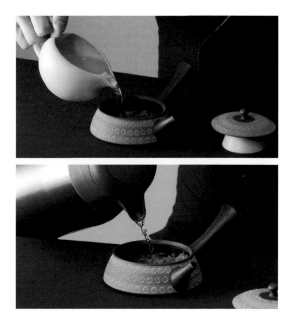

7

After three minutes, pour slowly around the edge of the cup. When the tea comes in contact with the hot surface of the cup, the aroma will emerge. You will only end up with a few drops of tea but the taste and favor will unfold explosively in your mouth, so sip it slowly, a little at a time.

How to enjoy the second and third steeping

Most of the *unami* is extracted in the first steeping so use hot water to extract a pleasant astringency and more of the aroma. Since a lot of leaves are used in this case, bitterness and astringency dissolve easily so make sure not to wait but pour the tea immediately into the cups. For the third steeping, you can pour straight from the kettle, but again make sure to keep the steeping time down to only a few seconds to fully enjoy a light and refreshing third steeping without excess bitterness.

How to Make Cold Brewed Sencha

Japanese tea makes an excellent beverage even when steeped in cold water

1

First, prepare a bottle, such as a cold infusion bottle, that has an inbuilt strainer. Put 15–20 g of tea leaves in the bottle and pour in about 750 ml of cold water. If you happen to be in Japan, most water is suitable for Japanese tea, but if the tap water in your area is hard, use a water softener or purchase bottled soft water.

2

It takes time to extract the taste and flavor of tea in cold water and some leaves will float to the surface. To bring out the best of the tea, tip the bottle upside down a couple of times and mix the leaves thoroughly before refrigerating. If you prepare it before going to bed, both the taste and flavor will be extracted to the maximum while you sleep. Otherwise, at least two hours will result in a fairly good cold brewed sencha.

Other suitable teas

Fukamushi Sencha (p. 21)

Gyokuro (p. 22) / Hojicha (p. 28)

Kukicha, Bocha (p. 29)

Steeping guide

Tea leaves **15–20 g**

Water **750 ml**

Steeping time **2 hours**
(about 8 hours, if possible)

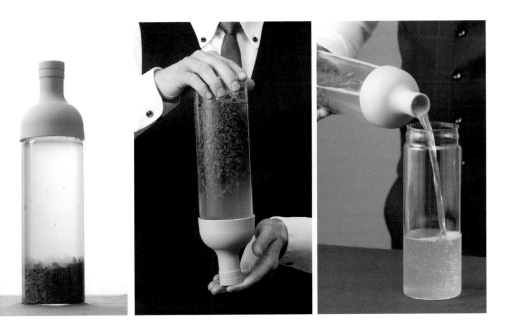

3

After refrigeration, the tea leaves will have sunk to the bottom of the bottle, making the clear layer on top paler and weaker in taste compared to the slightly cloudy liquor in the bottom. To even it out, turn the bottle upside down a few times.

4

When tea leaves remain too long in a bottle, harshness and excess astringency will inevitably occur. To avoid this, pour the contents into another bottle or decanter. If you do not intend to drink all the tea at one sitting, keep the remainder in the fridge but make sure to consume it within 24 hours.

How to Enjoy Cold Brewed Sencha

Enjoy cold tea from a wine glass

It might seem surprising but the best way to enjoy the aroma of cold brewed sencha is to drink it from a wine glass. White wine glasses are the most suitable for the purpose. In this way, you can enjoy not only the aroma but also create a special atmosphere of elegance. Trying it out as a "lunchtime wine" may well prove to be an unexpected way to come up with a great new food pairing.

How to Steep Gyokuro

How to best bring out the characteristic taste of gyokuro

1

In order to fully enjoy the *umami* of gyokuro, it should be steeped at low temperatures. First, prepare two water coolers to cool down the water.

2

Put the leaves in a small teapot or a small flat *hohin* (pictured) and spread them out evenly. Pour hot water from the kettle into the first water cooler.

3

The water in the water cooler will not only feel hot but will, in fact, be very hot, so in order to cool it down even more pour the water into the second cooler. Whenever you pour from one vessel to another, the temperature will drop about 10 °C.

4

After waiting for a while, hold the bottom of the cooler to test the temperature. When the temperature has reached around 50 °C (120 °F), pour the water gently into the teapot.

Steeping guide
Tea leaves **6 g**
Water **60 ml**
Water temperature **50 °C (120 °F)**
Steeping time **120 seconds**

5

Put the lid on the teapot and steep the tea for about two minutes. Pour it into each cup a little at a time and keep repeating this to adjust the strength. Since gyokuro is very thick and rich in *umami*, it is best enjoyed in small quantities from tiny cups. Make sure to pour all the liquor into the cups in order not to ruin the second steeping.

How to enjoy the second steeping

For the second and following steepings, raise the temperature of the water gradually. In the first steeping, *umami* plays the main part whereas in the second and further steepings it will weaken in favor of the unique aroma and sweet aftertaste of gyokuro.

Eating Tea Leaves

Good Japanese tea will also taste good when eaten. Gyokuro, in particular, with its soft leaves low in astringency, can be turned into a true delicacy after the third steeping. By pouring *ponzu*, a type of Japanese citrus sauce, or soy sauce on top of the used leaves, you will be able to enjoy the taste and flavor trapped in the leaves in a completely different way.

How to Whisk Matcha

Using a chasen to whisk matcha is the best way to bring out its natural flavor and taste

1

Before whisking, start by sifting the matcha. This step is often overlooked but is very important to avoid clumps forming during the whisking process.

2

Pour hot water into the bowl and soak the *chasen* (bamboo whisk), rinsing it as well as softening its tines. This makes it easier to whisk the matcha.

Preparation guide
Matcha powder **2 g**
Water **100 ml**
Water temperature **80 °C (175 °F)**

3

As with sencha, the taste and flavor change depending on the amount of tea used, the type of matcha, the temperature of the water and, of course, the tea bowl and how the tea is whisked. These can all be adjusted to suit your taste. In the case of usucha (or weak matcha), for example, whisking the tea to produce a fine froth reduces the astringency and gives the tea a smoother mouthfeel. Use your wrist to move the chasen back and forth as you would whisk eggs. However, if you want to enjoy high-quality matcha at its best, you can bring out the astringency and umami by mixing it carefully without producing froth.

Matcha has gained worldwide fame as an ingredient in lattes, smoothies and different sweets. High-quality matcha has a natural sweetness and is very enjoyable as it is without additives. A good matcha tastes excellent when drunk from a traditional Japanese Raku bowl or from a heat-resistant glass.

How to Steep Hojicha

Sweet roasted aroma—perfect after meals

1

First, put the tea leaves in the teapot. To best bring out the characteristic aroma and lightness, use fewer leaves than when you steep sencha. Since the leaves are lighter than sencha, take two full Japanese tea scoops or roughly four teaspoons to get four grams.

2

Spread the tea leaves evenly in the teapot. It might look like a small amount, but too many leaves will produce excessive bitterness.

Other suitable teas
Bancha (p. 26) / Kyobancha (p. 27)
Konacha (p. 30) *Using a tea bag

Steeping guide
Tea leaves **4 g**
Water **200 ml**
Water temperature **Boiling**
Steeping time **30 seconds**

3

Pour boiling water into the teapot. In general, the water is cooled after boiling when steeping Japanese tea. However, in the case of hojicha, the characteristic aroma is more easily extracted and better enjoyed when steeped at a high temperature.

4

Oversteeping will give the tea a harsh and bitter taste, so start pouring after 30 seconds. Pour a little at a time to obtain even strength in each cup. Although 30 seconds might sound short, it is long enough to extract the characteristic aroma of hojicha.

Bottled Japanese Teas

Foreigners visiting Japan for the first time are often surprised when they see how many Japanese drink green tea from plastic bottles. They probably have a vision of all Japanese carefully steeping their tea in traditional teapots. Following the release of canned and bottled versions of oolong tea and black tea, the green tea equivalent was finally introduced in 1985. The product, "Oi Ocha" by Itoen, greatly changed the way the Japanese consumed green tea. During the development stage there were a lot of hurdles, the most challenging being that the quality of steeped green tea alters very easily compared with black or oolong tea.

Oi Ocha
Unsweetened Green Tea

In particular, *ichibancha* (the first harvest tea) is prone to degrade after steeping compared to the more stable later harvests, and it was the latter that were eventually chosen as the raw material. Ascorbic acid (vitamin C) was also added as a stabilizer, and this proved to be the solution. In this way, a ready-to-drink tea beverage with no added sugar or other sweeteners was successfully created.

Considering the type of tea used for making the product, tea in plastic bottles can be interpreted as a modern version of bancha, greatly valued by many Japanese because it can be enjoyed anywhere. Some people worry that the convenience of bottled tea has made people forget the joy of steeping tea with teapots. In fact, there are many factors behind the reduced use of teapots among Japanese today. In the past, several generations used to live under the same roof, but with the household structure changing in favor of nuclear families and with more working women in society, tea drinking with the family has, to a large degree, disappeared. Moreover, the introduction of coffee, black tea and various carbonated beverages has diversified the market, thereby making green tea vulnerable to competition. If bottled tea did not exist, it is likely that there would be even fewer opportunities to come in contact with green tea in modern Japanese society.

Although devoted tea drinkers who use teapots might consider tea in plastic bottles a blasphemy, its very existence can also be thought of as evidence that the Japanese are not willing to give up on tea despite the rapid modernization of Japanese society.

Chapter Six
Japanese Teapots

How to Choose a Teapot

Choosing a teapot with a good design is, of course, important but since it is a tool made for steeping tea, functionality and good tasting tea are the major criteria. Stoneware teapots absorb bitterness and astringency to some degree, which makes the tea taste milder. Very porous ceramic teapots, on the other hand, will absorb even the aroma and are therefore not suitable for Japanese tea. White porcelain is not necessarily bad, but since it does not absorb bitterness or astringency to any notable degree it tends to give the tea a slightly sharp taste. From my experience, steeping Japanese tea in well-crafted stone ware pots from either Tokoname or Yokkaichi (Bankoyaki) generally gives the best result.

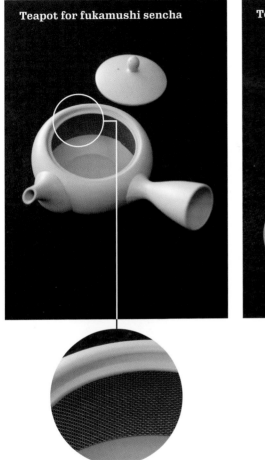

Teapot for fukamushi sencha

Metal strainer

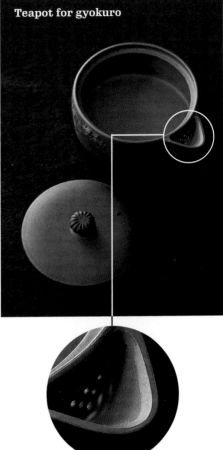

Teapot for gyokuro

Ceramic strainer

After considering the material of the teapot, the next thing to check is the tea strainer. A ceramic strainer with many holes makes it easier to pour tea but it is not a good choice when steeping teas with small particles, such as fukamushi sencha and konacha, since they tend to clog the strainer. For those teas, it is better to use teapots with a metal strainer. With gyokuro, which is steeped in small quantities at low temperatures, a small teapot called a *hohin* is most suitable. On the other hand, tea steeped at high temperatures like hojicha requires a thick teapot that will retain the heat so that there is no loss of aroma.

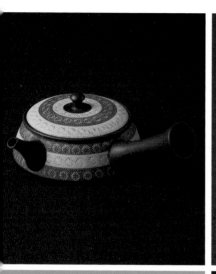

The Beauty of Japanese Teapots

"Tea is for drinking, not for looking at"
The Tokoname Black Tea Set

To drink tea from thin white porcelain is considered by many people to be the standard. This way of enjoying tea has its origin in China, just like tea itself. However, tea is something that we enjoy more with our palate than with our eyes. This sentiment is fully expressed in a new kind of black stoneware tea set that has been developed at a well-known pottery in Tokoname city in Aichi prefecture. Contrary to conventional thinking, the color black was chosen on purpose

so that the color of the liquor cannot immediately be seen. This makes it completely different from most other teaware. Moreover, the heaviness of the cups resembles that of Raku tea bowls, the Japanese hand-molded, lead-glazed earthenware originally invented in Kyoto in the 16th century especially for the tea ceremony. To hold a Toko-name cup highlights not only the presence of the utensil but also of the tea itself. In the world of matcha, there is the tea ceremony, a uniquely Japanese cultural practice. However, in the case of sencha ceremonies, influence from continental Asia is apparent. In modern days, we have finally seen a genuinely Japanese tea drinking culture take form. By bringing to life a completely new way of enjoying Japanese tea, this Tokoname tea set seems to push this even further. It might very well be a game changer.

Afterword

During my high school years I became interested in Japanese tea. In my search for information. I came across *The Book of Tea* by Kakuzo Okakura, written over a hundred years ago, in which he explains the Eastern mindset through the lens of tea culture. Okakura states that, although Westerners show little interest in Eastern culture, they have wholeheartedly accepted the Eastern practice of drinking tea. Today's world, where globalization is progressing rapidly and intercultural exchange has become more common, is very different from the world Okakura lived in. Even though many Westerners are still enjoying tea in a rather superficial way, more and more people across the globe are becoming interested in Japanese tea despite geographical and language barriers, which can pose significant hurdles. Because of this, for many years I have strongly felt that the time is ripe for a new book in the field of tea.

Japanese tea is not simply a beverage. It is extremely multifaceted with its long history and the complex cultural practices that surround it. Moreover, tea brings people together regardless of nationality. It deepens our understanding of other cultures and thus helps to patch the gaps between us. In this way, I believe that tea drinking can help us build a more peaceful world. By attempting to translate the beauty of Japanese tea into words, I sincerely hope that more people will graduate from superficial tea drinking and more fully enjoy the wonder and benefits it has to offer.

Finally, I would like to thank you for taking your time to read *A Beginner's Guide to Japanese Tea*. If it serves as a gateway to the wonderful world of one of the most fascinating and complex beverages, I could not be happier. I also hope that this will inspire people and lead them to enjoy Japanese tea in a way that suits them. From the bottom of my heart, I hope that Japanese tea will enrich your life just as it has enriched mine.

Profile
Per Oscar Brekell

Born in Sweden in 1985, Per Oscar Brekell developed an interest in Japanese tea during his high school years, which grew into a passion that led him to relocate to Japan.

In 2010, he studied at Gifu University and in 2013 returned to Japan to work for a Japanese company. He became a certified Japanese tea instructor in 2014, completed an internship at the Tea Research Center in Shizuoka and has been working for the Japan Tea Export Council. In 2018, he set up his own business and is now involved in tea education projects overseas and in arranging tea events and seminars in Japan. He is the first non-Japanese to receive a certificate for making handrolled sencha, and in 2016 he was awarded the CHAllenge Prize by the World Green Tea Association.

"Senchaism": Per Oscar Brekell's Tea Selection

Japan is abundant in good tea but what I find most intriguing and fascinating is single estate Japanese tea. As I discussed in Chapter 3 (see pages 48–59), sencha can have many different tastes, from floral, herbal and fruity to forest-like notes, all depending on the cultivar. The degrees of flavor elements like *umami* and astringency also differ. Given this diversity of tastes, sencha can be enjoyed just like a fine wine or a single malt whiskey. Refined single estate and single cultivar Japanese tea came into existence only about twenty years ago, and thus the production volumes are still small compared with blended teas. However, this relatively new phenomenon clearly shows the potential of Japanese tea, and is what makes it truly special. For someone like me, who greatly values my teatime, I think this type of tea is by far the most enjoyable. For this reason I started the brand "Senchaism" to put emphasis on single estate Japanese tea with the aim of enriching more people's lives. My hope is that it will be enjoyed not only by the Japanese but by tea lovers from all corners of the world.

Glossary/Index

Acknowledgments

A number of people deserve my appreciation for their help in making this book possible.

First and foremost, I would like to thank Kentaro Ishibe, a renowned tea critic and pioneer in the field of single estate Japanese tea. He is tireless in his effort to gain and share knowledge in the field, and without his contributions I could never have completed this extremely challenging task. I am indebted for life for all the inspiration, knowledge and guidance that have led me to my current position.

I would also like to thank Ako Yoshino for her invaluable perspectives on the Way of Tea as well as her advice in the field of history.

Yoshi Watada, a notable tea sommelier, stands out as one of the most meaningful encounters in my life, and I will never forget the first time he brewed tea for me. Not only did he open my mind to the seemingly infinite ways of enjoying Japanese tea, he also introduced me to many of my most important partners.

Katsumi Tsukiji, for cultivating and processing the tea that changed my life, I thank you. When I had my first sip of Tobetto, I instantly knew that life would never be the same again. Your memory will live forever, engraved in the hearts of tea lovers in Japan and elsewhere.

I would also like to express my thanks to all individuals and organizations who contributed photographs. Thanks to all the images, this book truly came alive.

Teruyuki Isobe, Yoshikawa Setsudō and Kazufusa Katō Shūkei and Seiji Ito Jinshū for your superb craftsmanship. Without your outstanding teapots, Japanese tea would not be the same.

To my dear tea friends Marzi Pecen and Noli Ergas, for correcting my English, I thank you both.

I would also like to express my thanks to the editors, designers and everyone else involved at Tankosha, the publisher of the original Japanese version, who without doubt worked very hard to make this book possible.

Many certified Nihoncha instructors took great care of me when I was new to Japan. Among them, I would especially like to thank Yasuhiro Ogasawara for making my year in Shizuoka possible, and Yoshiko Atsumi, who provided me both with valuable connections as well as many social skills necessary for navigating the world of Japanese tea.

I would also like to thank everyone who took care of me during my internship at the Tea Research Center in Shizuoka Prefecture. Thanks to the detailed instructions of Hideyuki Katai and many other helpful researchers, both in the tea fields and in the factory, my one year as a trainee proved to be fruitful and productive beyond expectations.

To Mitsutoshi Sugimoto, for keeping me in Japan and for making me a part of the Japanese Tea Industry after my internship in Shizuoka, I thank with you with all my heart.

Yoshihiro Honda and Osamu Kondo have supported me in Japan far more than anyone could ever ask. Not only this book but many of my activities are made possible thanks to their financial support and their management. Thank you for always believing in me.

I would also like to thank everyone at Tuttle for discovering me and for taking on this project. As an admirer of Eastern culture since young, Tuttle books have for long been part of my life and it is a true honor to be part of the Tuttle family.

Finally, I would like to thank my family, friends, teachers and the thousands of people who supported and believed in me.

Credits

Design
Hiromi Kutsuma

Photos
Yukiyo Daido
Kentaro Ishibe
Hayato Motosugi
Per Oscar Brekell
Namiko Ikeda (National
    Institute of Fruit Tree
    and Tea Science, Japan)
Shizuoka Prefecture Tea
    Research Center
Kakegawa City
Tea Industry Chamber of
    Kagoshima
Mitsuhiro Inokura (TEA
    FARM INOKURA)

Ako Yoshino
Ren Yamagata
Yamamasa-Koyamaen
Aoi Ueda
BIZENYA Keiichiro Shimizu
Tea Industry Promotion
    Association of Shirakawa-
    town
Akihito Takaki
ITO EN, LTD
Tea Industry Chamber of
    Kagoshima
Minami-kyushu City
Hiroshi Okamoto
Chachanoma Omotesando
IPPUKU&MATCHA
GOCHIO cafe

Shutterstock l norikko
    (front cover – green tea)
Shutterstock l 7maru
    (p. 66, top right)
Dreamstimes l Sarun
    Ongvanich (front cover
    – tatami texture back-
    ground)

Editorial Assistance
Kentaro Ishibe
Ako Yoshino
Marzi Pecen
Noli Ergas

"Books to Span the East and West"

Tuttle Publishing was founded in 1832 in the small New England town of Rutland, Vermont [USA]. Our core values remain as strong today as they were then—to publish best-in-class books which bring people together one page at a time. In 1948, we established a publishing office in Japan—and Tuttle is now a leader in publishing English-language books about the arts, languages and cultures of Asia. The world has become a much smaller place today and Asia's economic and cultural influence has grown. Yet the need for meaningful dialogue and information about this diverse region has never been greater. Over the past seven decades, Tuttle has published thousands of books on subjects ranging from martial arts and paper crafts to language learning and literature—and our talented authors, illustrators, designers and photographers have won many prestigious awards. We welcome you to explore the wealth of information available on Asia at **www.tuttlepublishing.com.**

Published in 2021 by Tuttle Publishing, an imprint of Periplus Editions (HK) Ltd.

www.tuttlepublishing.com

BREKELL OSCAR NO BILINGUAL NIHONCHA BOOK
Copyright © 2018 Oscar Brekell/TANKOSHA
English translation rights arranged with Hobby Japan Co., Ltd. through Japan UNI Agency, Inc., Tokyo

English Translation © 2021 by Periplus Editions (HK) Ltd.

Library of Congress Control Number: 2021944195

ISBN 978-4-8053-1638-2

Distributed by
North America, Latin America & Europe
Tuttle Publishing
364 Innovation Drive
North Clarendon, VT 05759-9436 U.S.A.
Tel: (802) 773-8930 | Fax: (802) 773-6993
info@tuttlepublishing.com
www.tuttlepublishing.com

Japan
Tuttle Publishing
Yaekari Building, 3rd Floor
5-4-12 Osaki, Shinagawa-ku, Tokyo 141 0032
Tel: (81) 3 5437-0171 | Fax: (81) 3 5437-0755
sales@tuttle.co.jp | www.tuttle.co.jp

Asia Pacific
Berkeley Books Pte. Ltd.
3 Kallang Sector, #04-01/02,
Singapore 349278
Tel: (65) 6741-2178 | Fax: (65) 6741-2179
inquiries@periplus.com.sg
www.tuttlepublishing.com

Printed in Malaysia   2108VP

25 24 23 22 21   6 5 4 3 2 1